CW01304286

SOZO

for

Professional Counselors

Copyright © 2013 Margaret Nagib

All rights reserved.

ISBN-13: 978-1493563159
ISBN-10: 1493563157

DEDICATION
to Jenni

Contents

ONE: Introduction to Sozo   **23**
- Sozo's Theoretical Model

TWO: Ministering to the Spirit and Restoring the Soul   **31**
- Wholeness is a Biblical Principle
- Study of the Soul

THREE: The Tripartite Nature of Man   **43**
- The Body
- The Soul
- The Importance of Soul Health
- The Human Spirit
- Why the Human Spirit is so Important in Counseling
- The Interaction and the Divinely Intended Order

FOUR: A New Assessment Tool: The Divine Order   **61**

FIVE: What is Sozo?   **73**
- The Father Ladder
- Viewing the Father Ladder from a Psychological Perspective
- How to Use the Father Ladder/Sozo in Psychotherapy
- Jenni and the Father Ladder

SIX: Psychological Backing for Sozo   **101**
- Ethical and Spiritual Interventions in Psychotherapy
- Attachment Theory
- Prayer and Forgiveness

F.A.Q.   **118**

ACKNOWLEDGMENTS

Many thanks go to my "spiritual mommas" Dawna DeSilva and Teresa Liebscher for impacting my life, my future, and my work as a clinical psychologist forever. Words cannot express the impact the two of you and your ministry has had on me and countless others.

Many thanks also go to my professors at Wheaton College who taught me and guided me towards excellence in the integration of faith and psychology.

Thank you Meier Clinics. I am forever grateful for the wonderful and supportive training ground and Christian community you provided.
I owe much of who I am as a clinician to my time spent there.

And finally, a special thanks to Timberline Knolls Residential Treatment Center. It has been an amazing privilege to work with the brave residents there and to be trusted by Timberline to create it's Christian Program which is the first of its kind to integrate Sozo principles.

Note to the Reader

Sozo for Professional Counselors is designed as a supplement to the Basic Sozo materials. It is written for **professionals** who are interested in bringing the power of God into their work by integrating Bethel Sozo but it will also benefit **non-professionals** who are interested in how psychology and inner-healing interact. It is based on my own experience with using Sozo in outpatient and residential treatment settings for several years and how I have personally come to understand how Sozo prayer and psychotherapy can interconnect. My hope is to highlight how psychology and Sozo complement each other and at times challenge each other with an emphasis on how I as a psychologist view Sozo from my professional lens. This book is based on the presentations I give around the country to professionals and non-professionals on wholeness, as well as the Sozo trainings I offer as the International Bethel Sozo Director for Professional

Counselors. These Sozo trainings are geared specifically for professionals working in the mental health and allied fields.

Forward

Several years ago I packed my forest green Chrysler Neon with everything I owned and made the long trip from the 'burbs of New York City to the 'burbs of Chicago to begin a new adventure and fulfill my dream of pursuing a doctorate in clinical psychology. During that new season, I cried out to God on many occasion with this one request, "God, help me to be a *really*, good therapist."

I saw becoming a psychologist as not only a career but as a vocational calling and ministry. So I chose the best Christian graduate school I could find that could specifically train me in the integration of my Christian faith and the pursuit of psychological wholeness.

As I began the 7-year quest to become an effective licensed clinical psychologist, I quickly came to love my new school, studies, and professors. Three months into my time in Chicago, a senseless tragedy struck my immediate family. I do not believe that a loving God ordains such tragedies to grow us, but I do remember the words of my prayer haunting me in the days, weeks, and months to come as I attempted to carry on with life and graduate school, "Do you really want to be a good therapist?"

The words that were once made as an almost desperate request from an eager, bright-eyed 21-year-old turned into an invitation from God to pursue my own wholeness at any cost in the midst of a confusing, devastating, and life altering loss that shook my vocational, existential, and theological beliefs to the core.

By the time I graduated 5 years later, I had learned more about how to be "a good therapist" from my journey with God in understanding the pain of what my family and I had been through (and personal therapy) than in all of my formal studies. But the timing of it all was uncanny because in parallel to Holy Spirit growing and teaching me, I had also been learning from the best in Christian psychology about how to walk alongside people in their pain and mental illness to restore health and vitality. When I officially began my clinical work after graduation, I remember the thrill of stepping into a part of my destiny that was in fact so fulfilling. I had become an effective Christian clinical psychologist and I loved my work.

On the next leg of my journey in trying to understand the integration of faith and psychology for myself as a Christian and as a therapist, I wanted to know how to bring a deeper level of wholeness to my clients. Ten years after graduation, with a foundation of experience and confidence in my clinical and relational skills, new questions began to gnaw at my heart and cross my lips during my quiet times with God. "What does it take to get fully whole and am I called to 'treat' the human spirit?"

Despite the growth and healing I had witnessed over the years I began to question the concept of wholeness because on some levels my faith and my psychology seemed to be in conflict. The scriptures told me God had the power to heal anyone and anything but my psychological training kept me abreast of all the limitations to psychological health and wholeness.

In my quiet time with God one day I heard Him say, "You know, your Christian psychology is really good at getting at the soul. You are really good at sitting with people and helping them make sense of their mind, their will, and their emotions. And because of that, they are able to do things they weren't able to do before. But what happens when you just reside in the realm of the soul? What happens when you never help them connect with their spirit? What if their soul gets so "big" that they don't connect with their spirit and they don't even know how to live out of their spirit?"

A parallel process was occurring with God and me. The psychological concept called "parallel process" occurs when a process or dynamic that is on one level in an individual's life also plays out on another level. As I began probing Him for deeper levels of healing and wholeness, He began teaching me about the human spirit, Holy Spirit, and the need for my own spirit to be awakened in a fresh way. This new question was catalyzed by a passage of scripture.

> **Ephesians 1:18-21:** I pray that the eyes of your heart may be enlightened, so that you will know the hope of His calling, what are the riches of His glorious inheritance in the saints, and the incomparably great power for us who believe. That power is the same as the mighty strength He exerted when he raised Christ from the dead…" (NIV)

The words of this powerful passage, which I had overlooked so many times in the past, began to haunt me. God began to highlight the truths therein that I needed to fulfill my new spiritual and vocational longings. The **same power** that raised Jesus from the dead was available to me as a believer. Personally, I had to admit that I had an unsatisfactory experiential understanding of the depth of this promise, but I soon found that all I had to do to change this reality was to ask.

So I began to pursue this powerful promise, and in that pursuit, Holy Spirit led me to Redding, CA. The journey that began in 2008 with the question, *What does it take to get fully whole—body, soul and spirit?* led me to Bethel Sozo in 2009. It has been an integral part of my work with clients ever since. My own personal need to grow in my ability to connect with my own spirit and the Spirit of God triggered a 2-year hiatus from the clinical world. With God's leading, in September of 2009, I enrolled in what I now affectionately call "Holy Spirit School," more formally known as Bethel Supernatural School of Ministry in Redding, CA.

One

Introduction to Sozo

In February of 2009 I attended a conference at Bethel Church in Redding, CA. While visiting their bookstore, I came across training materials about their inner-healing ministry called "Sozo." Sozo was unlike anything I had ever heard of before in my 15 years of clinical experience in the Christian psychology realm. I was intrigued by the idea that because the healing work of Sozo relied solely on the work of God's Spirit, it could be expected to bring about complete restoration for body, soul, and spirit.

The ministry's claim to have seen countless numbers of people with various mental health conditions restored was also intriguing since Sozo is a lay ministry and not therapy. Many of the testimonies even involved conditions that the psychological world has deemed at best "manageable."

As a psychologist, this piqued my interest, and on the long flight back to Chicago, I listened to the training tapes. That next week, I returned to work to find a former client of mine scheduled to see me after a year-long hiatus from treatment. She is a young married woman who had been in treatment prior to this for five years. I treated her for a severe eating disorder that included bouts of starvation, self-induced vomiting, and exercise addiction. This client's case was so severe that she required both partial hospitalization and intensive outpatient care. Her treatment team consisted of me as her psychotherapist, a psychiatrist (MD), and a registered dietitian.

After much hard work, she had gained a measure of health and told me she was ready to terminate therapy and venture out on her own. And although I knew there was much more work to be done and that she was far from being cured—if she ever would be—I honored her measure of progress and her need to test the waters for herself.

After exchanging a brief synopsis of the past year, Jenni told me she was coming back to counseling because she wanted to "go to the next level" in her eating disorder work. But what she really wanted to know was if I could help her go to the next level in her relationship with God. I thought about the Sozo training tapes I had just listened to a few days earlier. I felt Holy Spirit nudging me as if to say, "Do it!" So despite my internal argument with Holy Spirit that professionals "just don't do these things," I told her about the new things I was learning and asked her if she wanted to give it a try. She courageously agreed and we scheduled her to come in for a special session— a Sozo session.

> **Sozo's theoretical model is based on the idea that emotional wounds from our past create false beliefs about ourselves and our relationships with others. In turn, these false beliefs create blocks in our relationship with the Godhead.**

Much to both of our surprise, Jenni came out of our three-hour session that day feeing completely healed of her Anorexia and Bulimia and I came out having witnessed the power of God to heal like I had never seen before in my life. Jenni's life completely changed as she began connecting with God on a deeply intimate and personal level like she had never experienced in her whole life as a Christian.

In the coming sessions, it became evident that Jenni's eating disorder symptoms, thoughts, and behaviors were dramatically changed. The focus of therapy quickly shifted after her Sozo session to issues of living in her newfound freedom, restored identity, and more intimate relationship with the Godhead. Now, years later, Jenni continues to report how that one session changed her life forever.

> **My days of helping others in my own professional knowledge and strength alone were over and my new role of creating a space for Holy Spirit to work through me to heal my clients had begun.**

It has been over 4 years since that life-altering event for Jenni. She continues to be free from what tormented her and has gone on to live her dream—a dream that had been biologically near impossible when she was in the throes of her eating disorder. Jenni is the proud mother of two children. I was forever changed after that session as well and began the task of trying to process for myself what I had witnessed with the knowledge that my clinical work would never be the same. I remember reflecting on the session immediately after Jenni left the appointment that day and emphatically wondering, "What in the world have I been doing for the past 10 years?!"

My days of helping others in my own professional knowledge and strength alone were over and my new role of creating a space for Holy Spirit to work through me in order to heal my clients had begun.

Sozo's Theoretical Model

In a nutshell, Sozo's theoretical model is based on the idea that emotional wounds from our past create false beliefs about ourselves and our relationships with others. In turn, these false beliefs create blocks in our relationship with the Godhead—Father, Son, and Holy Spirit.

The premise of childhood wounds creating faulty mental constructs that are integrated into the psyche creating problems later on down the road, was no new concept to me as a psychologist. This historically proven, psychologically sound, and well researched principle is involved in almost every theoretical model in contemporary psychology and is the basis for many of our most popular psychotherapies. What I found to be unique about Sozo, however, was how this framework specifically took into consideration how these wounds and resulting constructs specifically related to an individual's relationship with God the Father, Jesus, and Holy Spirit.

There is a fair amount of excellent writing on the theory of God attachment in the Christian and secular psychological literature. Sozo takes the idea of attachment and even God-attachment to a new level by not only identifying how our earthly attachments are mirrored in how we relate to God, but also removing the blocks in our relationship with God that are created by our earthly attachments. More about how attachment theory supports Sozo is discussed in the sixth chapter, "Psychological Backing for Sozo."

> **Sozo shifts the focus from talking about God in counseling, to helping the client directly talk with God.**

Two

Ministering to the Human Spirit and Restoring the Soul

I continued to offer Sozo sessions to my therapy clients when appropriate and quickly came to find Sozo to be a practical tool to help me address the client's spiritual, physical, and psychological health. As I continued to use it with clients, one of the major differences I found was that Sozo shifts the focus from talking about God in counseling, to helping the client directly talk with God. It does this by making God as healer the focus of the session instead of the counselor as healer or even the therapeutic relationship as healer.

> **Some techniques appear (to most professionals) to be similar to psychodynamic and experiential psychotherapies; however, inner healing emphasizes prayer-filled encounters with Christ as the change mechanism instead of therapist mediated or psychological theory-derived activities.**
> Garzon, Worthington, and Tan, 2009 (p.115)

This was a challenging idea for me to embrace at first because traditional counseling is based on the premise of the therapeutic relationship as primary. Sozo by no means demeans this truth, but what I came to realize is that healing and transformation is more easily accessible when the presence and power of God is welcomed into every aspect of the counseling process—initial intake, assessment, treatment and aftercare.

> **Sozo shifts the focus from talking about God in counseling, to helping the client directly talk with God.**

When God is invited into the process in an intentional and active way, miraculous healing occurs. It occurs because you are accessing His power to heal and to transform lives, and You are inviting Him to do the work.

Matthew the disciple was careful to point out this very important truth about Jesus— that He paid the price for our complete healing through His death on the cross. "When evening came, many who were demon-possessed were brought to him, and He drove out the spirits with a word and healed all the sick. This was to fulfill what was spoken through the prophet Isaiah: 'He took up our infirmities and bore our diseases' (Matthew 8:16-17 NIV). This truth is no different today, and we can deliberately and in faith rest in and activate this truth in our approach to treatment with our clients.

> **When God is invited into the process in a deliberate and active way, miraculous healing occurs.**

Wholeness is a Biblical Principle

As Christian counselors, we have a unique opportunity to address not only the biological and psychological aspects of the person but to address the whole person—body, soul, and spirit—to promote wholeness. Jesus is our model for this (Isaiah 61), and Holy Spirit empowers us (Ephesians 1).

> **Isaiah 61:1-3** He has sent me to bind up the brokenhearted, to proclaim freedom for the captives and release from darkness for the prisoners, to proclaim the year of the Lord's favor and the day of

vengeance of our God, to comfort all who mourn, and provide for those who grieve in Zion—to bestow on them a crown of beauty instead of ashes, the oil of gladness instead of mourning, and a garment of praise instead of a spirit of despair. (NIV)

Ephesians 1:17-20: I keep asking that the God of our Lord Jesus Christ, the glorious Father, may give you the Spirit of wisdom and revelation, so that you may know him better. I pray that the eyes of your heart may be enlightened, so that you will know the hope of His calling, what are the riches of His glorious inheritance in the saints, and the incomparably great power for us who believe. That power is the same as the mighty strength He exerted when he raised Christ from the dead… (NIV)

Jesus came to comfort ALL who mourn (Isaiah 61:2). Then He commissioned us to do the same and even greater works than these (John 14:12). He equips us with the "hope of His calling," a "glorious inheritance," and dead-raising power. As He speaks to us through these scriptures, we recognize that what is available to us as believers and counselors is so much more than any treatment model or technique could ever offer. However, we first need to comprehend and apprehend this reality for ourselves. And that's what I had to do.

> **Faith actualizes what it realizes.**
>
> Pastor Bill Johnson

As stated earlier, the primary goal of Sozo is to identify and heal root wounds and cognitive distortions that hinder an individual's relationship with God. My parallel process included this. I needed to be healed of distortions I had that kept me from apprehending this reality and bringing it into my clinical work. My personal journey in this began with a new and more intimate connection with the person Holy Spirit and the re-awakening of my own spirit. Like Jennie, going "to the next level" in my own intimate experience with the Lord came with a life-altering encounter. On February 3, 2008 I was visiting a friend's church in Oak Park, IL when it felt like a veil was lifted and my spirit was activated in a fresh way. In my personal encounter that day I met "Freedom". Freedom had been there all along but it was as if I could not detect or interact with Him fully. The "eyes of my heart" were in need of enlightening (Ephesians1:18).

Midpoint in the sermon my ears perked up when I heard the pastor say, "If you are dissatisfied in your relationship with God, God has more for you." I immediately began to weep, my heart began pounding, and I felt the physical presence of Jesus standing behind me. I felt the pressure of a hand on my heart and a strange thought ensued in my mind. This thought was triggered by a physical sensation in my heart and emotions that I could not cognitively comprehend. It felt like there was freedom in the room and I could reach out and touch it.

> **2 Corinthians 3:16-18:** But whenever anyone turns to the Lord, the veil is taken away. Now the Lord is the Spirit, and where the Spirit of the Lord is, there is freedom. And we all, who with unveiled faces contemplate the Lord's glory, are being transformed into his image with ever-increasing glory, which comes from the Lord, who is the Spirit.

To address the needs of the spirit, we need to look to the scriptures. Traditional psychology primarily focuses on the soul by helping us to understand and address the needs of the soul. I believe this is why my counseling lacked the greater measure of God's power that I so eagerly desired. Even in my Christian psychology, I had come to rely more on my clinical knowledge and expertise.

> **In order to be aware of that consciousness union with God, it is necessary that everything be removed that hides that consciousness and dims the knowledge of God.**
> John G. Lake

As I will describe later, because psychology primarily focuses on the soul and the body, it can neglect to intentionally pursue the health of the human spirit. It may also fail to practically (in practice) recognize the role of the human spirit in connecting with God (talking about God instead of directly communicating with God and healing the blocks that keep individuals from a deeper ability to connect and receive from God).

Some might even argue that psychology was never intended to deliberately address the spirit and that spiritual interventions should be relegated to the field of spiritual direction or pastoral counseling and not psychology. However, the field of psychology is changing. The major governing board of psychology, the American Psychological Association (APA), is now actively promoting research in the area of psychology and spirituality. One of the nationally recognized researchers, Kenneth I. Paramagnet, PhD, leading the APA in this area states this:

> Psychologists are ethically obliged to be respectful and attentive to the cultural diversity of their clients, and religion and spirituality contribute to our personal and social identities. Finally, emerging research is showing that spiritually integrated approaches to treatment are as effective as other treatments. There is, in short, good scientif-

> ically based reason to be more sensitive to religion and spirituality in clinical practice. - (Pargament, March)

This is an exciting time in psychology for Christians in the field who are seeking to research and identify empirically-based therapeutic and spiritual interventions for healing. More about how the field of psychology is embracing spirituality and seeing it as **unethical to preclude spirituality** in a client's psychological care will be discussed in Chapter 6.

Study of the Soul

The Greek word for soul, psuche, is found in several places in the New Testament. A word study reveals that psuche (soul) is defined as the mind, the will, and the emotions. From psuche we derive the word "psychology", or in the original Greek, psyche logia which is translated "soul—logy." This of course fits with the field of psychology as we know it, for it is devoted to the study and science of the mind, behavior (will), emotions, and the interconnection of the three.

A Biblical understanding of wholeness according to involves letting God do the work.

> **I Thessalonians 5:23:** May God himself, the God of Peace, sanctify you through and through. May your whole spirit, soul (psuche) and body, be kept blameless at the coming of our Lord Jesus Christ. The one who calls you is faithful and He will do it. (NIV)

Christian counseling can involve partnering with God by intentionally making space in the counseling session for God to steer and orchestrate the healing work. Inviting God to do the work is one major way in which Christian counseling can be different than secular counseling. The word "sanctify" as it is used here means to "set apart" and "to make something different and distinct, breaking old associations and forming a new association" (Guzik). The emphasis is on the completeness of God's transformative work and His desire to set us apart as special and make us new. God's promise for wholeness and healing in this passage is powerful.

As treatment providers, it is important to understand this powerful promise and to understand the differences between our role and God's. Paul is reminding us that it is by *God's* power that transformation is accomplished and that He is faithful in accomplishing this goal. Our role as helpers is to bring this hope to our clients.

> **Matthew 11:28:** Come to me, all you who are weary and burdened, and I will give you rest. Take my yoke upon you and learn from me, for I am gentle and humble in heart, and you will find rest for your souls. For my yolk is easy and my burden is light (NIV)

We can assure and remind those we come alongside that no matter the difficulty or issues faced, God is faithful to heal them—body, soul, and spirit. If faith is the substance of things hoped for, then my therapeutic space is the place where my clients can encounter Jesus and His rest.

While, many treatment providers claim to address the individual's treatment needs "body, soul and spirit," what does this really mean and how do we as treatment providers do this? In the next chapter we will discuss the tripartite nature of man and the importance of addressing this in Christian counseling. It is important to note that like the mystery of the Holy Trinity, our tripartite nature functions as one and yet each aspect is unique and distinct from each other.

Sozo is a powerful tool that addresses the tripartite nature allowing God to do the work.

Letting God Do the Work

Jeremiah 6:16 "This is what the Lord says: '*Stand* at the crossroads and *look*; *ask* for the ancient paths, *ask* where the good way is, and *walk* in it, and *you will find rest for your souls*.' But you said, 'We will not walk in it.'"

Matt. 11:28 "Come to me, all you who are wear and burdened, and *I* will give you rest. Take my yoke upon you and *learn from me*, for I am gentle and humble in heart, and *you will find rest for your souls*. For my yolk is easy and my burden is light.'"

1 Pet 2:25 "For you were like sheep going astray, but now you have returned to the Shepherd and *Overseer of your souls*."

1 Thessalonians 5:23 "May God himself, the God of Peace, sanctify you through and through. May your **whole spirit, soul and body** be kept blameless at the coming of our Lord Jesus Christ. The one who calls you is faithful and *He will do it*."

Three

The Tripartite Nature of Man

We learn of the tripartite nature of man from the Bible.

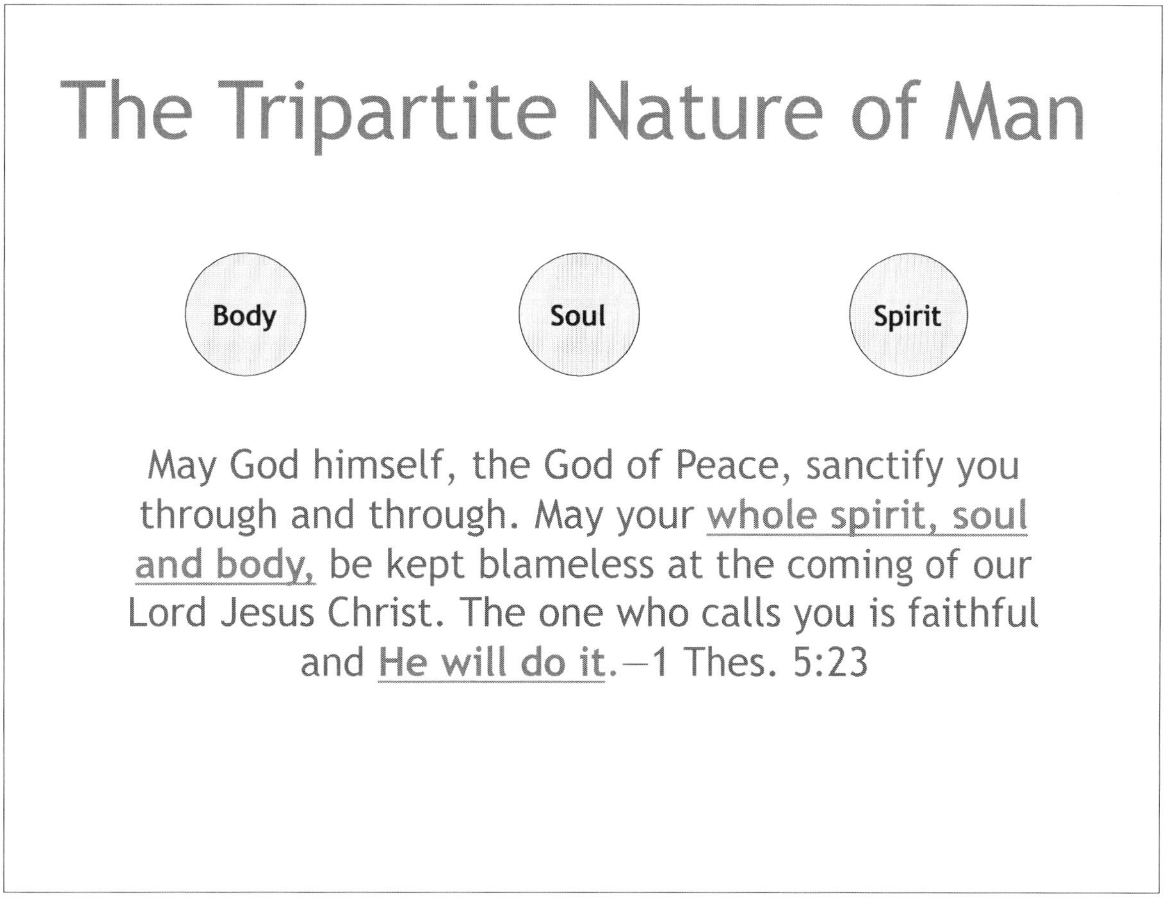

> # The Tripartite Nature of Man
>
> Body   Soul   Spirit
>
> May God himself, the God of Peace, sanctify you through and through. May your <u>whole spirit, soul and body,</u> be kept blameless at the coming of our Lord Jesus Christ. The one who calls you is faithful and <u>He will do it</u>. —1 Thes. 5:23

The body is the easiest of the three parts to understand. Its function is to "house" the soul and the spirit. The body is made up of the brain, nerves, muscles, organs, etc., and its primary function is to house our soul and spirit and give us awareness of the world around us. It is through the five senses— sight, smell, taste, touch, and sound—that we engage, interact with, and have conscious awareness of the material world. Without a body we would not be able to connect with what is around us. The five senses are the doorway to awareness and interaction between the body and the soul.

Over the past decades, the field of psychology has effectively increased in this understanding and has incorporated the importance of the body in the improvement of psychological health. Since the body and the emotions are intertwined, effective therapy guides an individual toward utilizing information from the five senses in order to discern thoughts and feelings. This is where expressive therapies such as dance movement and art therapy are helpful in connecting individuals with their body and their five senses.

Sozo utilizes this principle, with its emphasis on instructing the client to identify what they are sensing (in all five areas), and what they are thinking and feeling, because this information from the body and the soul is key to connecting with God's communication to them during the Sozo session and beyond. It is only through the spirit that the soul and body can fully interact with God, but it is our five senses, our thoughts, and our emotions that physically and psychologically interpret what is occurring spiritually.

> **Hebrews 5:14** But solid food belongs to those who are of full age, that is, those who by reason of use have their senses exercised to discern both good and evil. (NKJV)

We also now recognize as a field that mental disorders are connected with biology, and therefore proper psychological treatment requires an understanding of bio-chemistry, genetics, psychopharmacology, etc. Modern therapeutic interventions take this into account. Certain psychological issues such as eating disorders or addictions, for example, take a heavy toll on the body and the mind. It is helpful to discuss with individuals who struggle with such issues how psychological issues interact and affect their whole personhood, and particularly how these issues are being played out in the body.

(diagram below adapted from http://www.faithandhealthconnection.org)

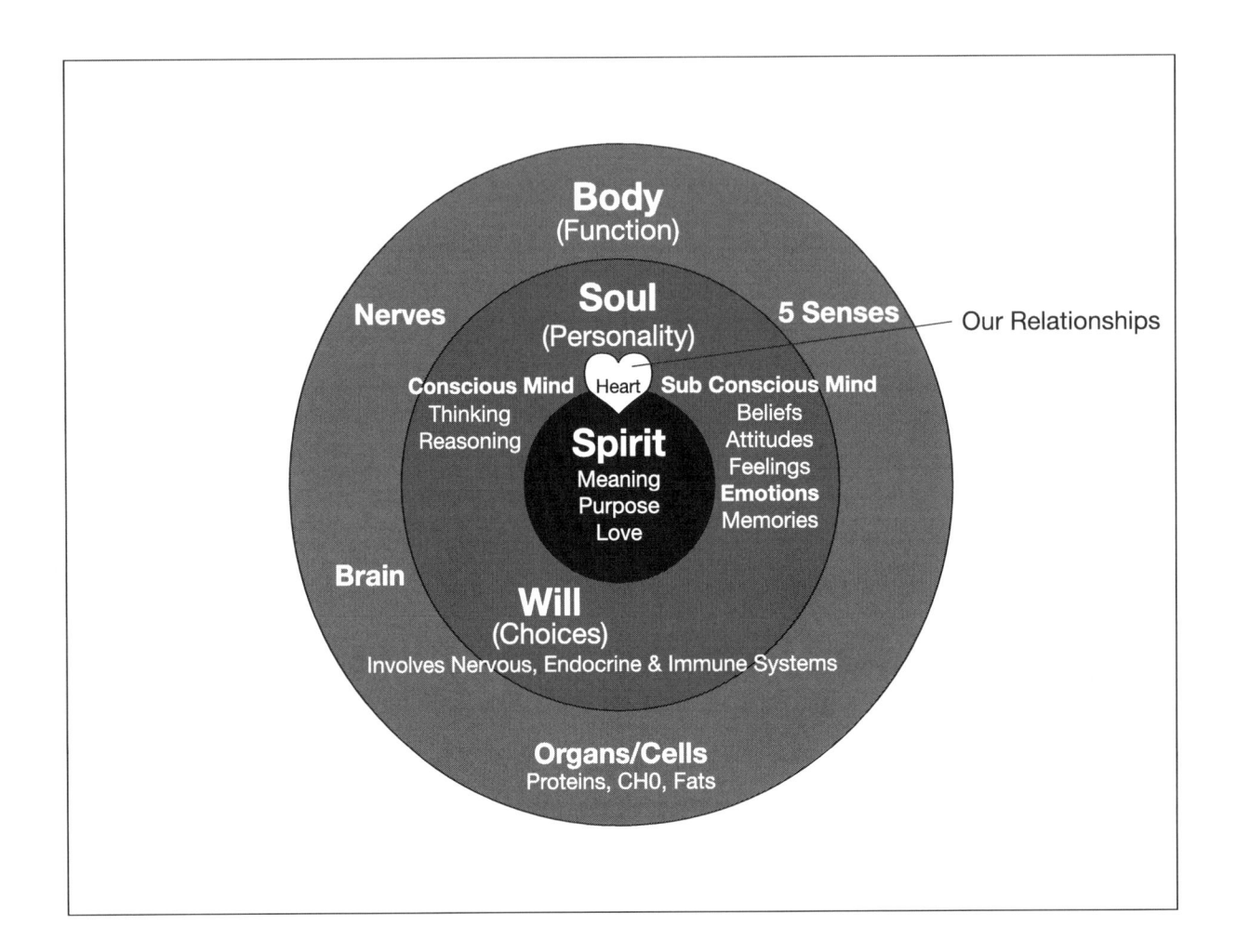

Body (Function)
- Nerves
- 5 Senses — Our Relationships
- Brain
- Organs/Cells — Proteins, CH0, Fats

Soul (Personality)
- Conscious Mind: Thinking, Reasoning
- Heart
- Sub Conscious Mind: Beliefs, Attitudes, Feelings, **Emotions**, Memories
- **Will** (Choices) — Involves Nervous, Endocrine & Immune Systems

Spirit
- Meaning
- Purpose
- Love

Psychiatry has also made significant gains in treating the biological aspects of mental disorders with medications and in helping us to better understand the role of genetics. The church can benefit from this knowledge. There are cases in which an individual may be suffering from psychological and even seemingly spiritual symptoms only to find that the culprit is a physical issue. Medical, genetic, and generational factors are addressed in a Sozo session by praying for physical healing and or generational deliverance of familial issues. However, Sozo does not assume all physical issues have a spiritual solution. This highlights the importance of utilizing spiritual discernment and clinical judgment to identify the true cause of a problem and then address the source of that problem accordingly. Professional counselors have the added benefit of being able to utilize clinical judgment and expertise along with spiritual discernment.

The *Body*

It is through the body that man comes into contact with the material world. Therefore, the body is that part which gives us consciousness or awareness of the world.

Body Trace: A powerful expressive therapy technique used by trained professionals to help individuals with eating disorders, body dysmorphic disorder, or trauma to recognize the distorted perceptions about their bodies, connect with their body in healthier ways, and gain a healthier view of self. The client is instructed to draw what they perceive their body to look like and to visually express the attitudes, emotions, and/or trauma held in their body on the paper. Later in the treatment process the individual is traced and the two are compared and contrasted.

The Soul

While the body gives us awareness of the outside world, the soul connects us with the internal world of thoughts, feelings, decision making, attitudes, beliefs, and behavior. It reveals the personality and allows us to be self-aware. Without a body the soul would only be conscious of itself. We know that if our thoughts are unhealthy, negative, or even distorted, this negatively affects our psychological health. But what many may not recognize is that negativity can also affect our physical and spiritual health. Since the soul acts like a mediator between the body and spirit, soul health is crucial to spiritual health. The soul as mediator means it can direct its attention to either the spiritual realm or the physical realm. It mediates between the spiritual realm via spiritual discernment and faith, and it mediates the physical realm via interpreting the information from the five senses.

The *Interaction*

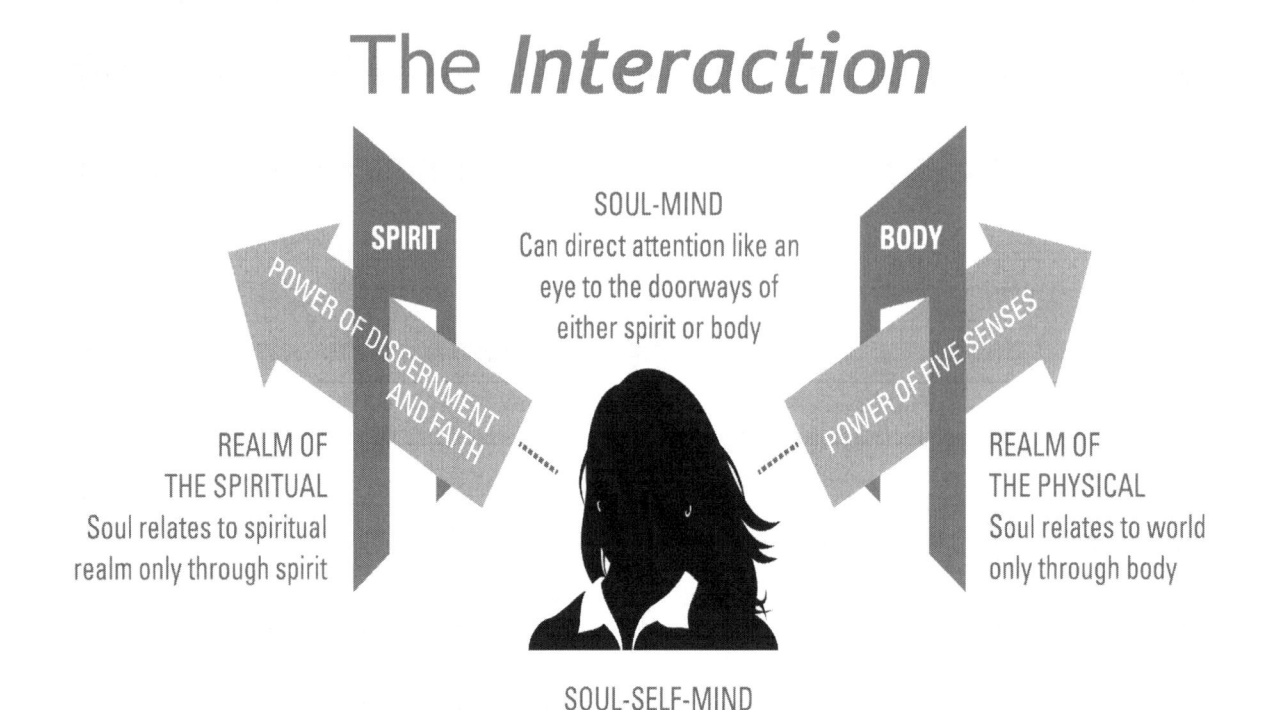

SPIRIT

BODY

POWER OF DISCERNMENT AND FAITH

POWER OF FIVE SENSES

SOUL-MIND
Can direct attention like an eye to the doorways of either spirit or body

REALM OF THE SPIRITUAL
Soul relates to spiritual realm only through spirit

REALM OF THE PHYSICAL
Soul relates to world only through body

SOUL-SELF-MIND
Without body or spirit, soul would only be conscious of self

The soul as mediator means it can direct its attention to either the spiritual realm or the physical realm. It mediates between the spiritual realm via discernment and faith, and it mediates the physical realm via interpreting the information from the five senses.

The Importance of Soul Health

The church can greatly benefit from psychology in the area of soul health. As stated earlier, it is only through the spirit that the soul and body can fully interact with God but it is our five senses, our thoughts, and our emotions that physically and psychologically interpret what is occurring spiritually.

Since the soul acts as a mediator, compromised soul health can negatively affect our ability to properly discern spiritual matters, which can impact our faith and theology. Distorted ideas about ourselves or the world due to psychological wounds can negatively affect our view of and/or experience with God. Poor soul health also affects our bodies. Inability to healthfully manage emotions, for example, can result in our bodies becoming sick or manifest psychologically-based somatic symptoms. Unresolved internal conflict, repressed anger or sorrow, can also cause problems in the soul that negatively affect other aspects of our being.

Paul highlighted the tension that we often experience between our thoughts, feelings, and behavior when he said, "I do not understand what

I do. For what I want to do I do not do, but what I hate I do" (Romans 7:15 NIV). The artwork on the following page was done by a residential treatment client in an art therapy session designed to help her connect with her body, soul, and spirit. She depicted this very dilemma and portrayed the battle she feels in her mind between her healthy thoughts and desires and her struggle with substance abuse and an eating disorder.

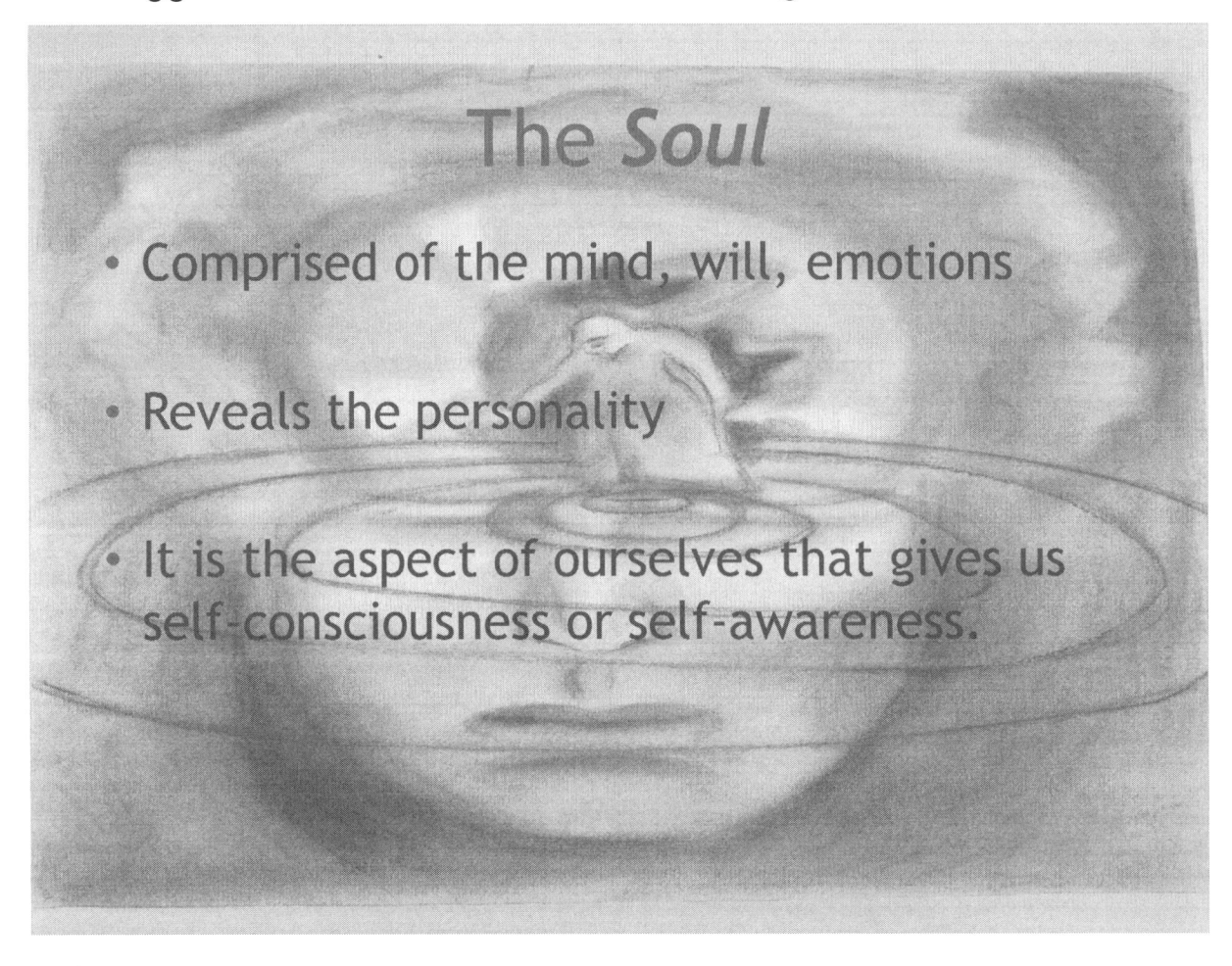

The *Soul*

- Comprised of the mind, will, emotions
- Reveals the personality
- It is the aspect of ourselves that gives us self-consciousness or self-awareness.

Art Therapy: a form of psychotherapy involving self-expression through painting, drawing, or modeling, used as a therapeutic activity or an aid to diagnosis.

The Human Spirit

And finally, "the spirit is that part by which we commune with God and by which alone we are able to apprehend and worship Him" (Nee, 1968).

John 4:24 states, "God is Spirit, and his worshipers must worship in spirit and in truth" (NIV). The Bible also tells us that Jesus perceived spiritual things in his Spirit (Mark 2:8). Our spirit gives us consciousness of God. It is that aspect of our being by which we apprehend such abstract things as love, meaning, and purpose.

> **We are spirit, we have a soul, and we live in a body.**

While the body connects us to the outside world, and the soul connects us to our inner world, the spirit connects us with the spiritual realm. In fact, it is only through the spirit that the soul and body can fully interact with God.

> **1 Corinthians 10:10-12:** But it was to us that God revealed these things by his Spirit. For his Spirit searches out everything and shows us God's deep secrets. No one can know a person's thoughts except that person's own spirit and no one can know God's thoughts except God's own Spirit. And we have received God's Spirit (not the world's spirit), so we can know the wonderful things God has freely given us. (NIV)

Much of the work of psychotherapy is spent mining the depths of our inner world to bring insight, direction, and healing. That is the main reason why it is so important to incorporate an understanding of the spirit and the role of God's Spirit in the Christian clinical world. God wants to reveal to us His deep secrets and the deep and precious secrets within our own heart and minds. He has equipped us to be able to do this by giving us His very own Spirit.

The *Spirit*

The aspect of our being by which we:

- Commune with God
- Apprehend and worship Him
- It tells us of our relationship with God
- God-consciousness

"God is Spirit, and his worshipers must worship in spirit and in truth." (John 4:24)

Jesus perceived spiritual things in his spirit (Mark 2:8)

Existential Psychotherapy: a philosophical branch of psychology that focuses on the client's inner conflicts regarding personal search for a meaningful existence, purpose, self-identity, and views around life and death. (artwork: Melissa Rocchi)

Why the Human Spirit is so Important in Counseling

If we are not careful, the work done in counseling can actually undermine an individual's spiritual connection with themselves and God by placing the emphasis on the soul (mind, will and emotions) over the spirit. While the work of the soul is important, this can cause an imbalance in the person in which their soul is strengthened by the process of psychotherapy, and the spirit is neglected or relegated to a secondary, tertiary, or even a non-existent role. Sickness in one aspect of our being affects the health of other aspects of our being. Likewise, healing in one aspect of our being can and does affect the health of another aspect but it is still worth noting the value of intentionally addressing all three uniquely and individually.

Body	Soul (psuche)	Spirit
Connected to the material world.	Connected to the internal world.	Connected to the spiritual world.
Communicates via the five senses.	Communicates via thoughts, emotions, and decision-making.	Communicates via faith and discernment

Without a spirit or body, our souls would only be conscious of self. And if the spirit is that aspect of our being by which we know and comprehend deep and heavenly things, why then would we not access this for ourselves and for our clients in therapy?

The Interaction and the Divinely Intended Order

One of the ways in which we can communicate the divine order to our clients is by the simple explanation that we are spirit, have a soul, and live in a body. Another way to say this would be: "God dwells in the spirit, self dwells in the soul, while senses dwell in the body" (Nee, 1968). The divinely intended order for the interaction of our tripartite nature places the spirit as the noblest part of man, occupying the innermost area of his being. The body is the lesser of the two. It takes the outermost place. The soul's role is critical and is primarily that of mediator between the body and spirit.

If you were to picture it like an organizational chart, the spirit would be the CEO and below the CEO would be the ancillary members of the body and soul. The divine order involves the spirit as CEO of the soul and body. The spirit's role is to communicate to the soul, and the soul exercises the body to obey the spirit order. Father God, Jesus, and Holy Spirit are the owners and board of directors. Sozo is like getting "memos" from the head office.

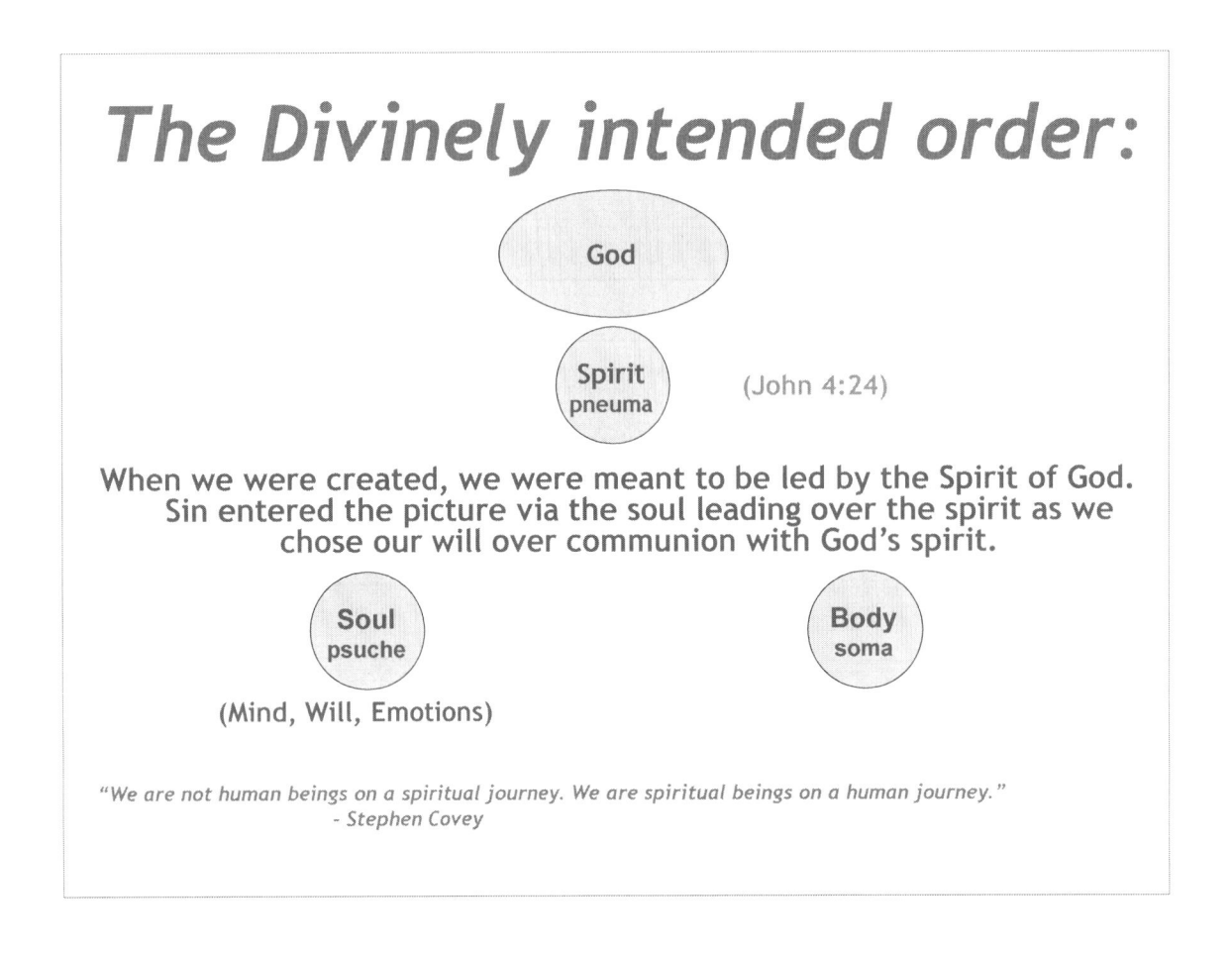

> # *The Divinely intended order:*
>
> **God**
>
> **Spirit** *pneuma* (John 4:24)
>
> When we were created, we were meant to be led by the Spirit of God. Sin entered the picture via the soul leading over the spirit as we chose our will over communion with God's spirit.
>
> **Soul** *psuche*   **Body** *soma*
>
> (Mind, Will, Emotions)
>
> *"We are not human beings on a spiritual journey. We are spiritual beings on a human journey."*
> *- Stephen Covey*

When we were created, we were meant to be led by the Spirit of God. This divinely intended order was interrupted when sin entered the picture via the soul eclipsing the spirit as we chose our will over communion with God's Spirit. "Though outwardly we are wasting away, yet inwardly we are being renewed day by day" (1 Corinthians 4:16 NIV). The mind and body are subject to blindness and decay, but the spirit is over them both. In counseling, we have the opportunity to invite God's Spirit to minister to the spirit of man as we recognize that God dwells in the spirit, self dwells in the soul, while senses dwell in the body.

> ***God* dwells in the *Spirit*,**
>
> ***Self* dwells in the *Soul*,**
>
> **while *Senses* dwell in the *Body*.**
>
> *Before the fall of man the spirit controlled the whole being through the soul.*

Four

A New Assessment Tool: The Divine Order

What happens psychologically and spiritually when the body is ruling over the soul and the spirit? Or what if the soul is ruling over the body and spirit? In other words, what if the Divine order is out of whack?

In **Matthew 26:41** Jesus cautions the disciples to "Watch and pray so that you will not fall into temptation. The spirit is willing, but the flesh is weak" (NIV). When the body is ruling over the soul and spirit, the psychological manifestations we see include things like addictions. Biological drives and cravings that have been hard-wired over time in the brain are powerful forces. When an individual is in the throes of an addictive cycle, the biological drives underlying the addiction are in control of the individual and this is often dramatically reflected in their addictive patterns of thinking, emotions, decision-making, and behavior. When this occurs the individual begins to look more like the addiction than they do themselves. It is like the addiction is holding their personality captive. I have worked with several parents of addicted children and in almost every preliminary session they ask, "What happened to my sweet child? It's like she is a different person!" And I tell them all the same thing. "This is not your child. That is the addiction you are talking to."

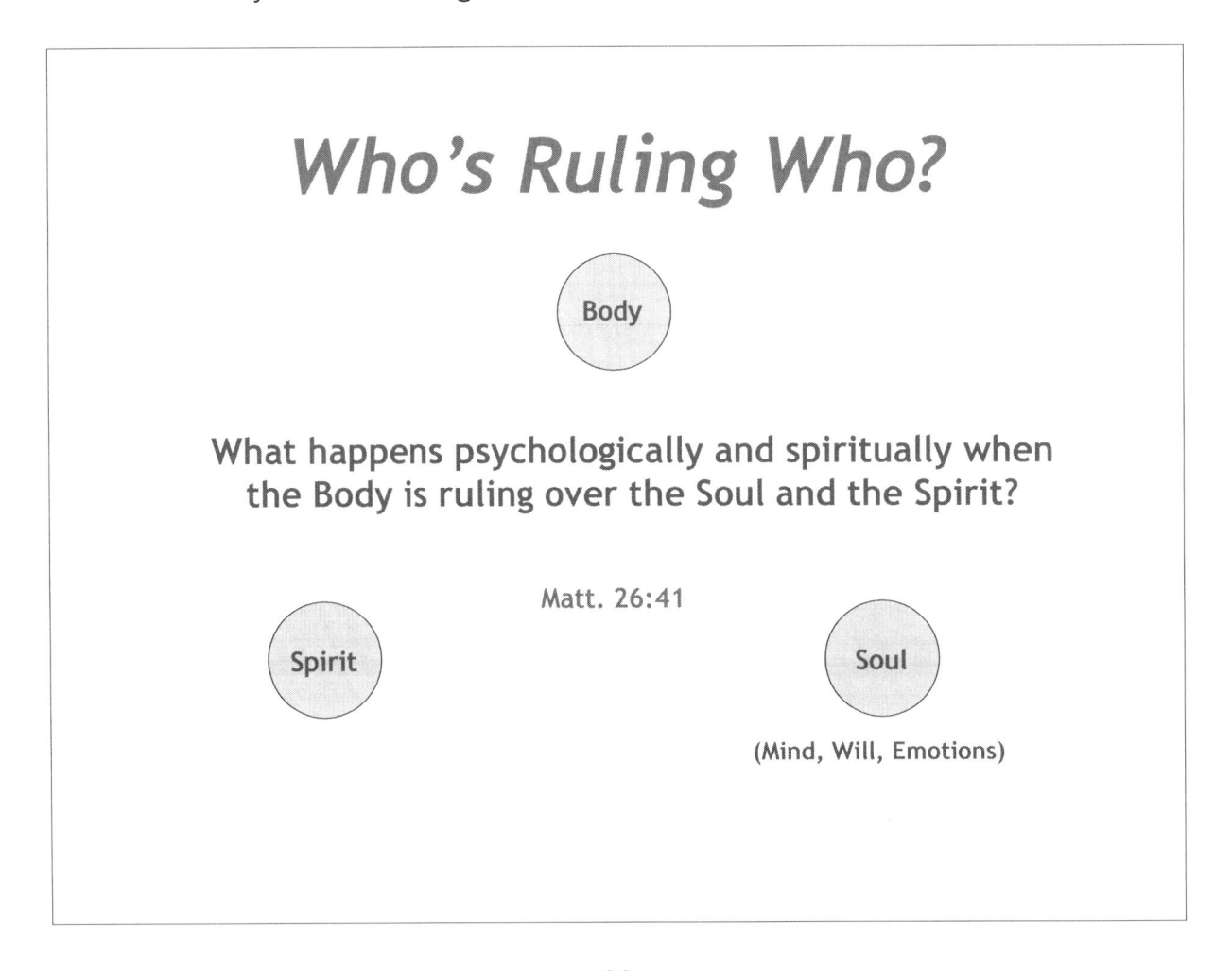

Who's Ruling Who?

(Body)

What happens psychologically and spiritually when the Body is ruling over the Soul and the Spirit?

Matt. 26:41

(Spirit)   (Soul)

(Mind, Will, Emotions)

Likewise, when the soul is ruling over the body and spirit, mood disorders such as depression, anxiety and OCD are evidenced as sickness in the soul begins to affect all other aspects of an individual's life. When our emotions or thoughts are allowed to take precedence over our spirit, this creates a life led by things like intellectualizing, perfectionism, distorted thoughts, excessive fear, anxiety, or an inability to regulate emotions.

The reality is mental illness affects all aspects because all aspects of our being are intertwined. However, it is helpful to both the clinician and the individual to begin to look at and separate out the unique effects on each part for healing to occur. Careful understanding of the tripartite nature of man and the Divine order helps us as clinicians to assess what is happening and how we need to intervene on behalf of the individual as a whole person. Each aspect of the individual needs to be identified and addressed. This involves seeing the Divine order as an assessment tool and asking the relevant questions when working to bring wholeness. What are the needs of this person's soul (mind, will, emotions)? What are the needs of this person's body? What are the needs of this person's spirit? What aspects of each are in need of healing, insight, education, etc.? How do I help this individual restore the Divine order?

Body Needs?	Soul Needs?	Spirit Needs?	Needs in relationship with God?

In addition to these needs, the Divinely intended order places God above us. To use the language of Alcoholics Anonymous, He is our "Higher Power." It is important to understand that wholeness is also compromised when there are issues that need to be repaired in our relationship or connection with God.

Jesus is our perfect model of healing. He healed and restored all who came to Him by touching their bodies, and in this process their souls and spirits were also healed. He saw the whole picture and when He restored individuals, He addressed each aspect of the person's being.

> **As we felt new power flow in,
> as we enjoyed peace of mind,
> as we discovered we could face life successfully,
> as we became conscious of His presence,
> we began to lose our fear of today,
> tomorrow or the hereafter.
> We were reborn.**
> (The Big Book of Alcoholics Anonymous, p.63)

The story of the woman in Luke 13 is a perfect example of how Jesus addressed the whole person:

> On a Sabbath Jesus was teaching in one of the synagogues, 11 and a woman was there who had been crippled by a spirit for eighteen years. She was bent over and could not straighten up at all. 12 When Jesus saw her, he called her forward and said to her, "Woman, you are set free from your infirmity." 13 Then he put his hands on her, and immediately she straightened up and praised God. 14 Indignant because Jesus had healed on the Sabbath, the synagogue leader said to the people, "There are six days for work. So come and be healed on those days, not on the Sabbath." 15 The Lord answered him, "You hypocrites! Doesn't each of you on the Sabbath untie your ox or donkey from the stall and lead it out to give it water? 16 Then should not this woman, a daughter of Abraham, whom Satan has kept bound for eighteen long years, be set free on the Sabbath day from what bound her?" 17 When he said this, all his opponents were humiliated, but the people were delighted with all the wonderful things he was doing.   (NIV)

Jesus was connected with God's Spirit when He spiritually discerned that the cause of this woman's physical ailment was spiritual and not physical. In verse 11 it states she was "crippled by a spirit" and in verse 16 Jesus says, "should not this woman . . . whom Satan has bound..." While I do not believe there is a demon behind every physical or psychological illness, it is clear here that for this woman the solution to her physical problem was not going to come by natural means.

Imagine for a moment this same woman living in modern times. She would have made an appointment with a specialist who would assess her condition and outline a medical treatment plan to address it. The fact that her ailment was actually caused by a spirit implies to me that medical intervention would not have worked for this woman. In the same way, how many times are we working with an individual and unable to effectively help them because we have failed to discern and address the possible spiritual causes of their presenting problem? Jesus effectively discerned that this woman needed spiritual deliverance to be able to experience physical healing. He was not, however, satisfied with just bringing physical healing via spiritual deliverance. Jesus's interaction with her shows He recognized the effect that 18 years of physical sickness had on her soul. Consider the host of cumulative effects that this spiritual problem had not only on this woman's body but also on her mind, will, and emotions. She was bent over. How did this affect her relationships with others and how they saw her? Think about how her self-esteem and self-efficacy were negatively affected. How was her relationship with God affected or her ability to worship Him?

Jesus addressed the negative effects on her soul when He (1) saw her and pursued her by calling her to himself in the middle of the synagogue, and (2) touched her. By doing this, He healed her soul and sent a powerful message to her and to the community in which she lived. She was seen. She was special. She was valuable. His actions communicated that she was important and deserving of deliverance, freedom, and wholeness. He reinforced this by restoring her identity when He proclaimed over her that she was, "a daughter of Abraham" (vs.16) whom Satan illegally kept bound for 18 long years.

Here is the perfect Biblical model of restoration to wholeness. Jesus restored her soul by calling her out in a public place and physically touching her, thereby providing her with a Divine encounter with **God** himself. He healed her **body** with the power of his verbal declaration by delivering her from the spirit that was oppressing her. Evidence of her spirit being healed came when "immediately she straightened up and praised God" and when Jesus verbally restored her **identity** as a daughter. This is the model that we as therapists can follow in our work with clients, and Sozo is a practical tool that reflects this model.

This passage shows us how the spiritual realm can affect every aspect of our being, even our ability to worship God fully. It powerfully displays the importance of spiritual discernment along with clinical expertise for proper diagnosis and treatment. In particular, the spiritual gifts of wisdom and discernment help us to understand the cause and determine the prescribed cure. Jesus exemplifies this in how he addressed the whole person. What a wonderful model to us as lay and professional counselors. 1 Peter 2:25 calls Jesus the "Overseer of your souls." This verse always makes me smile because I immediately think, "Jesus is a 'soul-ologist' too!" Throughout the New Testament, there are many examples of Jesus addressing the needs of the body, spirit and the soul when He healed a person.

It is undeniable that as Christian clinicians we can operate in a higher calling because "such confidence we have through Christ before God. Not that we are competent in ourselves to claim anything for ourselves, but our competence comes from God. He has made us competent as ministers of a new covenant—not of the letter but of the Spirit; for the letter kills, but the Spirit gives life" (2 Corinthians 3:5-6 NIV). We have the opportunity in every session to confidently release life, knowing that God's Spirit works through us and affords us His power to bring wholeness and restoration to every aspect of our clients' lives.

> **Very truly I tell you, whoever believes in me will do the works I have been doing, and they will do even greater things than these, because I am going to the Father.**
> **John 14:12 NIV**

As ministers of the Spirit of God, we can walk in confidence and bring life as we respect the tripartite nature—body, soul, and spirit and recognize that when one part is affected, the others are affected as well. We need help from God's Spirit and His spiritual gifts of wisdom and discernment to properly assess the problem and its solution. This allows us to become spiritually competent. And we can activate the power of faith in what Jesus already accomplished for us on the cross by praying in faith for physical healing or deliverance from oppressing spirits when necessary.

This is critical for our clients and our work with them. Vallotton and Johnson (2006) state it well. When we as clinicians or our clients "are ignorant or resistant to the spirit realm," we limit our "process, discovery, and prescription to single dimensional mind-sets; this produces only symptomatic cures, instead of true wholeness."p.231.

Thus by His Spirit, His power, and His word we can minister to the body, soul, and spirit of man. As intricate, complex, and perplexing our human problems can be in our tripartite nature, God's living and rhema word provides the ultimate in assessment, differential diagnosis, and treatment. His Spirit touching our spirit releases life and as our human spirit is activated, we carry His life and release it to those around us. Our human spirit, when connected to God's Spirit, is able to discern heavenly things and access God's perfect wisdom, truth, and knowledge. As Christian clinicians we can help our clients to not only strengthen their souls but to direct their soul's attention to the Spirit of God and toward the knowledge of heavenly things. Sozo is one of the best tools I know to accomplish this.

> **Hebrews 4:12:** For the word of God is living and active. Sharper than any double-edged sword, it penetrates even to dividing soul and spirit, joints and marrow; it judges the thoughts and attitudes of the heart. Nothing in all creation is hidden from God's sight. Everything is uncovered and laid bare before the eyes of him to whom we must give account. (NIV)

**But when touched by the Spirit of God,
a quickening takes place.
The spirit of man comes into activity
and begins to operate within him.
It not only discerns things in this life,
like the spirit of another, or in another,
but it reaches way beyond this present life,
and becomes that medium by which we know
and comprehend heavenly things.**
John G. Lake

Five

What is Sozo?

The Sozo ministry was founded in 1997 at Bethel Church in Redding, CA by Dawna DeSilva and Teresa Liebscher as a result of what they had experienced and learned over many years. Its founders credit the work of Randy Clark, Dr. Aiko Hormann, Pablo Bottari, Dr. Ed Smith, and John and Paula Sandford as influencing their knowledge and practice of inner healing.

> The Sozo ministry is a unique inner healing and deliverance ministry in which the main aim is to get to the root of those things hindering your personal connection with the Father, Son and Holy Spirit. Thus with a healed connection with Father, Son and Holy Spirit you can walk in the destiny to which you have been called (DeSilva, 2004).

Because there was such a miraculous difference in people's level of freedom often after experiencing only one session, the church team decided to begin sharing it with other churches and organizations. In the 16 years since it was developed, Bethel Sozo Ministries has traveled nationally and internationally to train and equip others. Many travel from all over the world to California to experience a session with the Bethel Sozo team at the church's lay counseling ministry, which is called the Transformation Center.

The Transformation Center does not make claims of being a professional counseling or diagnostic center and is not a licensed therapeutic facility but reports considerable success with complete healing of a variety of psychological problems with varying levels of severity including depression, anxiety, trauma, relationship problems and even Dissociative Identity Disorder. The importance of seeking professional help or taking psychotropic medications in adjunct to Sozo Ministry is not undermined. (Note: No quantitative or qualitative studies have been done to date of this publication to verify claims of miraculous healing or levels of freedom achieved.)

The Greek word sozo is found in the New Testament 110 times. The English translation of the word is "save" or be "saved." It is interesting that upon closer inspection of the Greek, sozo not only means "to save," but it has a deeper, multifaceted meaning. It also means, "to save, "to heal," and "to deliver." There is an exciting, deeper revelation of salvation that comes with this word study. The "sozo" work of Jesus' death on the cross was to accomplish not only salvation for souls but also healing for our bodies and deliverance for our spirits.

Sozo harnesses the full revelation of God's salvific power and promise. In Romans 10:9 we learn that Jesus died to save our spirits. "That if you confess with your mouth, 'Jesus is Lord,' and believe in your heart that God raised him from the dead, you will be saved {sozo}" (NIV). In Matthew 9:22, we see how Jesus heals our bodies, "But Jesus turning and seeing her said "Daughter, take courage, your faith has healed {sozo} you, and at once the woman was healed {sozo}" (NIV); And in Luke 8:36 we hear of Jesus' deliverance, "Those who had seen it told the people how the demon-possessed man had been cured{sozo}" (NIV).

Therefore, the goal of Sozo ministry is to not only bring restoration to a wounded soul, but to bring wholeness and restoration—body, soul, and spirit. This involves full recognition and application of what Jesus made available to us on the cross and restoration of an individual's relationship with God. Sozo also highlights the importance of the tripartite nature of man in relation to the unique needs of each part and how the distinct members of the trinity meet those needs.

The Father Ladder

There are four tools used in the Sozo session. The Father Ladder is the primary tool and is used to frame the session (All of the other tools flow out of the Father Ladder, so this will be the primary focus of this book). The Father Ladder is based on the premise that the ways in which we have been impacted by our earthly family and relationships affect our view of the Godhead and our (in)ability to feel connected and cared for by the Godhead.

The Sozo manual explains

> The first institution that God created was the family. This foundation represents the function of each of the Godhead (Father God, Jesus, and Holy Spirit in our lives. When our family members do not understand, or are unable to fulfill their roles in our lives, we have a misunderstood view of the Father God, Jesus and Holy Spirit. The Father Ladder is a tool that clarifies/emphasizes this connection to heal the wounds and lies that have been learned from our childhood. (p.6)

The framework of the Father Ladder describes the needs of the body as identity, provision, and protection; the needs of the soul as communication and companionship; and the needs of the spirit as comfort, nurture, and teaching. The needs of identity, provision, and protection are met by earthly fathers. The needs of communication and companionship are met by siblings and friends. And, the needs of comfort, nurture, and teaching are met by mothers. Likewise, the needs met by our earthly father are the same as the needs met by our heavenly Father. The needs met by our siblings and friends are the same needs met by Jesus. And the needs met by our earthly mother are the same as those met by Holy Spirit.

The "Father Ladder"
developed by Theresa Leibscher

Father	Identity Provision Protection *(body)*	Father
Jesus	Communication *(soul)*	Siblings/Friends
Holy Spirit	Comfort Nurture *(spirit)*	Mother

This framework helps to identify where an individual may have blocks to experiencing the fullness of the Godhead. For example, if needs such as provision, security, and identity went unmet in childhood, wounds and lies are created, and the individual will struggle to experience Father God meeting those needs in his or her relationship with Him. If the relationship with an individual's mother was not one of comfort, nurture, and guidance, his or her relationship and view of Holy Spirit is skewed by lies and wounds and may promote an inability to receive comfort and guidance from Holy Spirit. Likewise, relationships with peers and siblings play a significant role in how we see Jesus. If needs like companionship, friendship, and communication were not met, an individual will not believe Jesus can meet these needs. Thus, by repairing the wounds and lies that were created in our earthly relationships through the use of the Father Ladder tool, we directly impact our relationship with the Divine.

Through communication with God using simple questions, the areas of greatest wounding are identified, and through prayers of forgiveness the blocks between the Godhead and the individual are removed. At this point, the lies that the individual developed around himself, his needs, or around God are identified. The lies are audibly renounced, and the person asks God to replace the lies with His truth. What I observe time and time again as I take clients through this process is that a powerful connection between the mind and emotions is developed. This occurs as the individual is led to the point where he not only "knows" the truth, but reports emotionally experiencing it as true as he hears directly from God and begins to feel a greater connection with Him on several levels. This, of course, is a common goal in psychotherapy, but what is amazing about the Sozo process is how quickly clients obtain this level of healing and cathartic insight.

The Father ladder can be used to frame a session by either questioning the individuals about their relationship with their earthly families or by questioning them about their view of the individuals of the Godhead. The Basic Sozo Manual outlines the steps in detail.

Synopsis of the steps:

> 1. **Ask the individual how he or she views one or more members of the Godhead (Father, Jesus, Holy Spirit), or ask what he or she believes the Godhead thinks of him or her.**
>
> 2. **Have the individual forgive the member of the family that corresponds with one of the Godhead.**
>
> 3. **Have the individual renounce the lie that the Godhead will treat him or her the same way.**
>
> 4. **Make sure the individual is able to accept the truth that the Godhead gives him or her.** Sozo Manual p. 8

Viewing the "Father Ladder" from a Psychological Perspective

The theory behind the Father-Ladder is not dissimilar to popular psychodynamic, object-relations, and attachment theories that seek to identify wounds from early relationships that contribute to unhealthy patterns later in life. Once the wounds are identified during the Sozo process, the next step of identifying the lies and replacing them with the truth is typical of psychodynamic goals for personal insight and cognitive behavioral models that seek to identify cognitive distortions and reframe them with healthier more beneficial cognitions.

Instead of the traditional psychotherapy model in which the client and therapist process the past, Sozo is a dialogue between the Lord and the client with the therapist helping to facilitate the process. The therapist helps clients direct the attention of their soul (mind, will, and emotions) toward God through simple prayers that solicit dialogue regarding the wounds and lies that contribute to the blocks that they have within themselves and in their relationship with God. Sozo engages the soul but more importantly, it also engages the spirit in spirit-to-spirit communication with God. The body is also engaged as clients are encouraged to connect with their five senses in receiving communication from the Godhead and in discerning their physical and emotional responses throughout the process.

How to Use the Father Ladder/Sozo in Psychotherapy

It is generally recommended that the Father Ladder be used as it was intended and outlined by the Bethel Sozo ministry (see Basic Sozo Manual). Sozo was developed as a lay ministry designed to be performed within an established Sozo ministry context. This means that Sozo is NOT counseling. However, I believe the Father ladder is a valuable tool that CAN be used within the context of psychotherapy because it so clearly mirrors psychotherapeutic principles and is outlined by a clear replicable process.

Therapists who have been working with a client on a regular basis and have a good knowledge of the client's wounds from his or her family of origin may choose to start with the earthly family side of the Father Ladder. When working with a new client, it is usually beneficial to start with the Godhead side. When this is done, no lengthy intake is necessary because asking the client about his views of the Godhead will naturally provide projective material highlighting the client's wounds and dysfunctional attachments stemming from the family of origin. The Sozo process is also more reliant on God to steer the direction of the session. These are some of the practical reasons why a Sozo session provides an accelerated path to the healing process.

It is encouraged that if you are going to use Sozo in a clinical setting that you receive formal training and hold true to the model the way it was originally intended. Training involves attending a Bethel Sozo training and gaining competency in the model by receiving mentoring upon completion of the training. Holding true to the model means setting aside a special session with your client designated to go through the Father Ladder and the rest of the Sozo tools. The Sozo session usually takes two to three hours and is done in one session. It is recommended that a Sozo session be done in one sitting but it can be performed over several sessions depending on the nature of the clinical setting or the ability of the client to sustain a longer session. I have found that in my work with residential treatment clients, many are unable to handle an extended session because of the severity of symptoms combined with very low functioning. Therefore, multiple sessions are merited.

Once my clients have undergone a Sozo session, I train them to use the tools in their everyday lives:

> When going about your daily activities if you find yourself struggling with an uncomfortable emotion or have lost your peace in any way, ask Father God if there is a lie that you are believing. If you sense that the answer is yes, ask God to show you what event in your day contributed to that lie and if there is anyone that you need to forgive. Forgive the individual for his or her contribution to the lie you believed and whatever else God shows you. Renounce the lie and then ask God, "What is the truth?"

In a similar manner the Sozo tools can be used as needed within the session to promote ongoing connection to God in the process of psychotherapy as well as for addressing new wounds and lies that emerge. Often, this starts to occur naturally in the session as clients become familiar with the process and value the healing they receive and the opportunity to connect with God. Integrating aspects of the Sozo tools like the Father Ladder is a deliberate way to provide your clients with opportunities to connect with God in a supportive setting. It teaches them to rely on their connection with God instead of trying to handle the situation on their own or rely solely on you as their therapist.

Informed consent is very important when doing Sozo in a professional setting. Clients should be given full informed consent and made aware of the fact that Sozo was developed as a ministry tool and is a spiritual intervention. They can also be given the option of a Sozo session with their counselor, or with an outside Sozo ministry. If you prefer, you can refer a client to a local ministry for a Sozo session instead of performing the Sozo session yourself. Some therapists prefer this option because it has the clearest boundaries. The therapist does not have to be present. A third option involves referring the client to a Sozo ministry and sitting in on the session with your client. I know some psychotherapists who successfully use this third option and like it because of the flawless continuity of care. Both the second and third options involve cultivating relationships and finding trusted Sozo ministers who you can partner with in your area.

When and if to use Sozo with your client depends on a variety of questions:

- What is the client looking for in regards to treatment?

- Are they interested in or open to spiritual interventions? What have you ascertained from a spiritual assessment with the client?

- Would the client benefit from Sozo based on the presenting problem?
- What do you know about this client in regards to readiness and proper timing for a Sozo session? What clinical caveats or potential ethical issues should be considered?

- And of course, does the client want a Sozo session?

Following well-researched guidelines in terms of the integration of Christianity and psychology is very important in a clinical setting. The well-respected and renowned work of Dr. Mark McMinn thoroughly investigates and outlines guidelines for integrating faith, prayer, and Christian principles such as sin and forgiveness into psychotherapy. His book, which is a mainstay in Christian counseling graduate schools across the country, is a helpful resource. This is a particularly helpful resource for therapists have not been specifically trained in the integration of Christianity and psychology but seek to integrate Sozo into their work. Always use your clinical judgment and spiritual discernment in deciding when to utilize Sozo with a client, and seek supervision when necessary.

If I think a client can benefit from Sozo, I explain the Sozo process to them and present the ideas behind the Father Ladder and the other three tools. I then leave it up to them to decide if it is something they would like to participate in, and together we decide the appropriate timing.

As stated earlier, through communication with God using simple questions, the areas of greatest wounding are identified and through prayers of forgiveness the blocks between the Godhead and the individual are removed. **Sozo utilizes the power of forgiveness to bring resolution to these wounds.** The act of forgiveness is a spiritual practice and not necessarily a psychotherapeutic one. The Bible speaks of the power of forgiveness to release an individual from what has bound them and the freedom that results when we forgive "our debtors" just as He has forgiven us. Once the forgiveness occurs, the blocks between the individual and God begin to dissolve and the individual becomes more connected with God and able to receive His truth.

Jenni and the Father Ladder

During Jenni's Sozo session various roots of her eating disorder were identified. These were linked in part to a lack of safety and security in her relationship with her father that contributed to a sense of self that was strongly tied to performance and striving. Her father's lack of physical presence in the household due to his very important and high-powered job created anxiety in the household and a host of unmet needs for Jenni and the other members of her family, including her mother.

Jenni's mother dealt with her own anxiety by hiding behind a mask of perfection and the illusion that they were the perfect family. This only increased Jenni's anxiety and drive to perform and maintain her personal and familial facade. Her lack of true emotional connection with her earthly father left her insecure and without a sense of self-assurance. Her mother was of little comfort as her method of coping sent an unspoken message throughout the household that emotions like anxiety, dissatisfaction, sadness, or anger were scary, unacceptable, and not to be expressed openly.

The eating disorder became a solution. Jenni looked to the eating disorder to provide her with a sense of identity and to curb the anxiety that the insecurity created. These wounds were connected with several lies (or what we call in psychology cognitive distortions). One of the profound lies that Jenni believed was that she could never be good enough. Like good psychotherapy, the Father Ladder identified the root wounds and resulting cognitive distortions that contributed to Jenni's battle with Anorexia and life-long struggle with anxiety. The themes that emerged in Jenni's session were not completely unfamiliar to Jenni or me as we had identified several of them during her course of treatment. With that said, we were able to get to "the next level" of healing for her eating disorder and her desired connection with God at a faster pace and deeper level than ever before.

What I have found true time and time again is that when the Sozo process is applied, profound insights come to the forefront in a matter of hours instead of several sessions, weeks, or months. The unique aspect of the Sozo session is that the process of identifying and healing the root causes is done in direct communication and partnership with God. This is what causes it to be more efficient, effective, and therapeutically powerful. It's like psychotherapy on supernatural miracle grow. Plain and simple: God's communication, when invited into the counseling room, produces life. Proverbs 2:20-23 states, "My son, pay attention to what I say; turn your ear to my words. Do not let them out of your sight, keep them within your heart for they are life to those who find them and health to one's whole body. Above all else, guard your heart, for everything you do flows from it" (NIV). Unlike traditional psychotherapy or even traditional Christian psychotherapy, Sozo is ultimately psychotherapeutic communication with God.

Another unique aspect to Jenni's Sozo session was that God revealed to Jenni the unique spiritual factors that were contributing to her battle with her eating disorder. Like the woman who was bent over for 18 years, physical and psychological treatment interventions alone were not enough for Jenni to be set free from her eating disorder. As stated earlier, psychology calls the lies we believe cognitive distortions. They are rooted in the soul (the mind, will, and emotions) and suppress our true personality. These are different from spiritual forces that war against our spirit. Both affect our sense-of well-being but must be addressed differently.

Half-way through Jenni's Sozo session I heard Father God say to me, "Ask Jenni to ask me what the eating disorder looks like to me (God)." With eyes closed Jenni asked Father God to show her what the eating disorder looked like to Him. When Jenni did this, it was as if someone turned on a horror movie inside of her head. The words barely left her mouth when she became visibly distressed and fearful as she described a horrific black figure walking with her in the forest preserve that she regularly frequented at the height of her eating disorder. Jenni spent hours walking at this forest preserve as part of her addiction to exercise, and I remember in previous sessions we had discussed another reason why she loved to go to the forest preserve. She loved to go to the forest preserve because it was there that she could "be alone" with him. We had been using a metaphor in psychotherapy that at the time fit best. Jenni and I used to call her eating disorder "Ed" (acronym for Eating Disorder). Ed was her friend. Ed was her confidant. Ed was the one with whom she "cheated on" her husband. Ed was the one who got all of her time, all of her energy, and all of her affections. Only God could show Jenni the reality of what she was experiencing in the forest preserve. Anyone who treats individuals with eating disorders or who has a loved one who struggles knows you can tell the person until you are blue in the face that the disorder will kill them. But it is extremely difficult to actually get them to believe that.

After Father God spoke to her about what she was seeing, Jenni opened her eyes. She then looked me squarely in the eyes and proclaimed with resolve,

"I'm done. Margaret, I'm done with my eating disorder."

"Done?" I said with reservation. "Really?"

"Yes," she said. "If you saw what I saw you would be done too."

At that point in the session, Jenni was able to break off spiritual ties with her eating disorder. The spiritual alliance that she had made with Ed was at last broken. It was broken forever.

With her permission, I've included Jenni's first-hand account of her Sozo session:

March 4, 2009. A day I will never forget. The day that my Father God showed Himself to me in a way that was so tangible, so full of love, so powerful...I will never ever be the same.

Allow me to give some background. I have been in therapy for anorexia nervosa for the better part of 5 years. Margaret and I have worked hard to unravel the many facets that my eating disorder has employed to keep me in a death grip. I began seeing her at a time when I knew something was wrong in my mind but I was not aware of the true struggle. As one who desires to please others and "do the right thing," I knew I needed a Christian counselor to make things right. I believed she would just tell me what to do, I could comply and things would go back to "normal" (What is normal? I thought I knew...). But that is not how it works. The answers do not come from Margaret. The answers to the puzzle in which I found myself in would come from me as I did the work. Margaret would listen to me as I sat on her couch session after session, month after month, spilling my thoughts in an attempt to "make it through the session." Of course, I was not fooling her, but with patience she listened to my story and understood things about me and my eating disorder that I was unable to see clearly for myself.

Anorexia is a powerful disease. Completely in its grip, I believed myself to be powerful and safe. As Margaret and I continued meeting, the eating disorder grew stronger and Jenni became almost non-existent. My entire day revolved around meeting the demands of the tyrant in my mind; keeping the anorexia satisfied seemed my only purpose for existing.

Eventually, I went through an intensive hospital program for treatment. Not desiring to let my eating disorder go, I complied with the treatment to keep people happy. Unfortunately, because I was not really there for me this certainly did not mark the end of my tireless struggle. I knew I should want to be free of anorexia, but honestly it seemed like my only source of strength and identity. My faith did not waiver, I never doubted God's sovereignty but I did wish that He would just reach down and pull me out of it. My walk with Jesus suffered as I found myself unable to pray feeling guilty and dark. Always a pleaser, I knew that He knew the dirty secrets of my eating disorder and believed He was sick of it and sick of me.

As time wore on and progress was made with Margaret I desired more life and less eating disorder. We were working hard on unraveling the distorted thought processes and learning about my rigid ordered life and the core beliefs I had grown up with. I felt like I was more in control of the eating disorder and was able to "manage" it. (Obviously, my thoughts were still distorted. This is not a disease that plays second fiddle.) Still wanting to hang on to the anorexia but too scared to let it go, I did believe that it had lost some of its grip. Two steps forward, three steps back...and on and on. This was my life, right? I settled. I believed I would continue in my life making do with this monster in the closet. This was the "thorn in my flesh" I had come to accept it. My physical health slowly returned to normal and I felt OK, like I was out of danger and therefore in less need of regular therapy. So I stopped seeing Margaret on a regular basis and pretty soon months had gone by without a session.

I had began attending nursing school and during my last semester we studied psychiatric nursing. All of a sudden, I felt very vulnerable as the realization set in that this eating disorder was still at large. I decided I was finally ready to really work on this. Enough is enough. I went back to see Margaret. I was afraid she would judge me, and I was all ready to apologize to her. Of course, there was no need to apologize. Margaret knows that the course of recovery is not straight forward and that it can take many years and many stints in therapy to recover from such a powerful disease. Comfortable, and so safe back on her couch, I confessed I was ready to really work hard. I wanted to be free, not to settle any longer. She was encouraged to see my enthusiasm! That session went very well and I looked forward to meeting again, only I had no idea what my Father God has in store for me!

March 4, 2009. I remember when Margaret came to get me out of the waiting room She said, "I am really excited about our time today." I agreed and she asked me what I was excited for. I explained that I felt more motivated than ever before to get to the bottom of this. She asked if we could do an exercise in our session. She had just been to training in California at a church and wanted to try something new. "Yes, of course!" I was excited. She told me that in training she had learned a prayerful technique called Sozo. She explained that Sozo is Greek for "salvation, deliverance and healing." We began. She asked me to take a minute and consider the three personages of God: Father, Son, and Holy Spirit. She was ready with paper and pen to capture what I said and asked me to start with "Father." Tears came to my eyes. The first thing I said was, "I feel guilty." I felt like I did not know Father God, like I could not put into words how I saw Him. Margaret encouraged me to take my time. I remember saying a silent prayer, apologizing to Father God that I seemed to have negative images and impressions coming up. Then I began to say what came to mind and Margaret recorded:

- Father
- I feel guilty
- Aloof
- Chief Webber (A character on the TV show Grey's Anatomy who is distant, disconnected, and busy)
- Caring but distant
- Easier to disappoint Father God than Jesus
- I need an intercessor to get to Father God, not very approachable, impersonal
- Tends to be annoyed with me
- He loves me but He has the whole universe to worry about
- No face

Next, we moved on to the Holy Spirit and Margaret recorded:

- An extension of God, but I don't have a personal relationship with Holy Spirit
- I know He is there, but there is a disconnect – He is aware of me, but I feel unaware of Him
- Disconnected
- I picture an assembly line of workers, and the Holy Spirit is the assistant supervisor (with a clipboard), very busy, constantly moving, difficult to pin down or get attention of, pushing for work to be done a certain way and faster

Next, we focused on Jesus. He was by far the easiest for me to describe and get a feel for. Margaret recorded:

- There is a split within me, part of me feels like He can take the fact that I keep falling short, but part of me feels I am grieving Him.
- He has to forgive me again
- I want to be better for Him
- He loves me
- He does not seem aloof
- Frequently I feel He is sad and disappointed in me

When we finished that part, Margaret explained that God the Father, Son, and Holy Spirit have perfect community within themselves. When God created the family in Eden, its perfect design was to emulate the perfect community within the trinity. Father God represents <u>protection</u>, <u>provision</u> and <u>identity</u>; Jesus is <u>communication</u> and <u>friendship</u> and the Holy Spirit represents <u>nurture</u>, <u>comfort</u> and <u>teaching</u>. In our human families our father was created to provide <u>protection</u>, <u>provision</u> and <u>identity</u>; our mother was created to provide <u>nurture</u>, <u>comfort</u> and <u>teaching</u> and our siblings and/or close friends provide <u>friendship</u> and <u>communication</u>. Obviously, as a result of the fall, the human model is imperfect resulting in missing pieces and wounds from unmet needs. She then told me that eating disorders result from "father wounds". This was hard for me to hear. What does it mean? Margaret asked me to describe my relationship with my eating disorder. Without hesitation I told her that the Anorexia was my "bodyguard". Somehow I felt so safe and untouchable when I was surrounded by my eating disorder. I felt powerful and accomplished. I loved being a "good girl" for my anorexia. I felt taken care of and known. Clearly, I felt protected and provided for and had an identity: one of accomplishment and a good girl. Amazing.

Margaret asked if we could focus on God the Father in this session. She explained that how I described Father God would shed light on my impression of and feelings toward my own dad. She read the list that I had given her about Father God back to me. I felt all this guilt rise up in me that somehow I had seen my dad as perfect, and yet on some level was very aware of the deeper unmet needs that I had decided to ignore and resist. I did not like this. Margaret and I talked about how no human father is ever perfect and could never perfectly meet all of our needs. We talked about ways that I had defended myself against these wounds. I realized that for most of my life I have always wanted to stay on my dad's good side and be the good girl, to play by the rules, to be perfect. My dad worked very hard and provided a wonderful home for us. Because of his long hours he was not always able to be with us. Whenever feelings would come up that I wanted my dad, that I needed him, I learned to numb those out because feeling disappointed with him did not match my "perfect dad" belief. The eating disorder provided for my unmet needs. It helped me rise above the fear that my dad was not perfect. The eating disorder created a wall of protection, in reality, a prison. Margaret asked me to close my eyes and ask Father God to show me my wall. Immediately, I was standing with my nose up against a light colored cinder block wall stretching as far as I could see in both directions in a straight line. The ground I was standing on was white gravel. No color at all in this world. Margaret asked me about the wall, was it strong? Could I push it down or climb over? With my eyes still shut, I explored my wall. It is very strong, impossible to push down and way too high to climb over. Then I noticed a couple of cinder blocks missing a few feet down from where I was standing. So I went to explore and as I stood on my tiptoes I could barely see that on the other side of the wall there was green ivy growing. Interesting. Margaret explained that my wall was strengthened by unforgiveness. I needed to forgive my dad for the ways he unintentionally fell short in providing what I needed. She led me through powerful prayers to Father God confessing my need for protection, provision and identity and my quest to have those needs met outside of Him. Margaret helped me to pray through specific wounds and core beliefs that I have been living under all of my life. Using my list about Father God and my dad I prayed through tears releasing unforgiveness and disappointment.

Next, Margaret asked me to close my eyes and return to my wall. I asked Father God to take me back to my wall, and immediately, I was back at the cinder block wall again only this time there were more holes in it and I could see what looked like what I can only imagine the Garden of Eden looked like. I saw beautiful lush green plants and trees, sunshine filtering through and precious animals peeking out from behind the trees and plants. She asked me if I could push the wall down yet. No, it is still too strong. We needed to do some more prayers of forgiveness. She asked me to ask Father God what else I needed to forgive my dad for. A few more prayers through tears and I felt like I had released my dad from disappointment and unmet needs. So, Margaret asked me, "Are you ready to let go of your eating disorder?" When she asked me that I felt overtaken by intense fear. "No, I can't. I'm so scared to let go!" I cried for a couple of minutes feeling fear like I had never felt before. As I write this I realize I cannot capture the pictures Father God was showing me on paper. I only wish I could describe the intensity of those moments! Margaret then asked me to ask my Father God what He had for me in place of this intense fear. The eating disorder was at its very core intense, crippling fear. What does Father God have for me? So, with my eyes closed, I went to my Father God and asked Him, "Father, what do you have for me instead of fear?" Immediately, I was in this beautiful paradise setting. I was standing alone on a sandy beach dune overlooking the ocean at sunset with a sweet-smelling peaceful ocean breeze all around me. To make sure that I got His message, out over the water in a sparkling cloudy haze the word SERENITY appeared. My Father has perfect peace for me—beyond fear, beyond my hateful controlling "friend" anorexia where the world is dark and uncomfortable. My Father has a blissful peace of serenity <u>just for me</u>. Broken and with uncontrollable sobs I cried out, "It's too good! How can He have this for me? Why would He give this to me?" Margaret quietly said, "Ask Him." So, I did. I asked, "Father, how can this be? I am such a mess. How can you have this just for me?" His answer came like a fresh whisper. As I was standing on my beach he said, "Look around." So I looked and down the beach on either side of me stretching on forever were seashells—all shapes, sizes and colors, everywhere. He then said to me so tenderly, "My daughter, each of these shells that stretch on for eternity represent something that I love about you." Clear as day, His voice in my soul. If only I could show you this beach, this beach for Him and me. I felt His love in that moment, His grace like never before. It is not because of anything I have done. He loves me because

He loves me. My whole life I have believed in God's grace from an intellectual standpoint, but have always struggled at the heart level really believing that I can do nothing to gain His favor, to merit His grace and in an instant, I felt His love and grace lavished upon me. Again, Margaret gently asked me if I was ready to let go of my eating disorder. "I can't," I cried. "I want to, but I feel powerless to do it. I don't know how." She asked me to close my eyes again and describe how I saw my eating disorder. Again, the image was immediate. I see a rickety piece of drift wood in an ocean. I hold on to the drift wood to stay afloat, to stay alive. To me it is a life line. To anyone else it looks unsafe, unreliable and scary. Off in the distance is a huge yacht. I know my life is on that yacht, yet I feel powerless and terrified to let go of my drift wood. I am scared to let go and swim towards the yacht, towards life. Interestingly, this was a picture that Margaret and I had come up with years earlier when I was in a deeper struggle with the eating disorder and even still this was the immediate image that came to mind when asked what my Anorexia looked like. "I can't let go. What will happen to me if I do?" Margaret entreated, "Ask Father God how He sees your eating disorder." Still holding on to my "precious" drift wood, I asked Father God, "Father, how do you see my eating disorder?" I was immediately taken from my drift wood and felt as if I had entered hell. There was a cold darkness, a lifeless forest of stick trees. No green, no leaves. There was even terrifying music playing. All of a sudden, I saw a huge black web in this forest of brown, cold stick trees. As I moved toward the web I saw the most horrifying being I have ever seen in my life. And within the web there was a motionless body staring ahead without life, as if suspended in this place of darkness and evil. The eyes were black, and within them a story of utter despair, hopelessness, shattered dreams and loneliness. Then I realized this suspended shell of a person was me! And not only that, I realized this picture of me in a web was me right then, for this lifeless body and I were dressed in the same clothes. This is how Father God sees me right now; still completely held back and in bondage to the eating disorder. Even though I had felt like I was pretty free of the eating disorder, my Father, in His mercy showed me this evil, satanic stronghold. This was no rickety little piece of wood; this was bondage and utter despair. Margaret later told me that as I was describing this place to her the look on my face was so powerful, so real that my whole countenance betrayed the dark secret in my mind; the dark reality of my eating disorder that Father God in His grace and mercy allowed me to see for the truth of what it really is. As I was describing how scared I felt, how real this image of me suspended in a black evil web with lifeless eyes was, a voice instructed me, "Get out! Tear yourself free! You are a daughter of the King! Run for your life! God's armies are ready to deliver you!" So I did! I broke out of the web and I ran for my life, towards my life. As I ran, the forest started to change and all of a sudden I was in the "Garden of Eden" that I had seen on the other side of my wall. My wall was gone! I opened my eyes. The room seemed different, lighter… warmer… I looked at Margaret and in almost a whisper I declared, "It's gone, Margaret. It's gone."

I am delivered! I am set free! My Father God delivered me, set me free and I experienced His love, His tangible touch and voice like never before. I go to Him boldly now. I know where to go for protection, provision and identity—to Father God; for communication and friendship—to Jesus and for comfort, nurture and teaching—the Holy Spirit. I can pray and ask with boldness for any need. My spiritual life has never been the same. I have experienced what it means to be set free from an evil bondage, a prison, a walled-off existence. I have learned to forgive my parents, to release them from unrealistic expectations of perfection and being able to meet every need. I have grown in my love for them and am grateful for the wonderful gifts from God that they are.

In subsequent sessions, Margaret and I did process my relationship with the Holy Spirit and Jesus. The eating disorder was primarily resulting from a father wound; however there were areas that I needed to seek forgiveness for relating to my Mom. I am so thankful for the freedom that is found in forgiveness and authenticity.

Margaret will never know how grateful I am to her for her diligent and patient and God honoring counsel that she has provided for me. The Lord led her to California because He had something so amazing for her. She has obeyed His calling and is an instrument for the Holy Spirit to change lives. My anorexia was the biggest challenge of my life (so far), and while it was the most difficult battle and the most confusing struggle, I would never wish my life without it. Without it I may never have experienced my Father God in such an intimate and tangible way. I may never have experienced such a powerful deliverance. My husband, Scott, has been by my side throughout this whole ordeal. His strong and patient love consumes me, and I am so grateful to my Father for him.

Six

Psychological Backing for Sozo

Ethics and Spiritual Interventions in Psychotherapy

The question I get asked by Christian therapists the most when speaking on the above principles or when giving a Basic Sozo training is, "Is it ethical to use Bethel Sozo in my practice since it is a spiritual intervention and not a psychological one?" My answer? According to the American Psychological Association (APA) it is unethical to work with a client and not assess the client's spirituality, respect their religious beliefs and practices, or address the importance of their spirituality to their daily lives and presenting problem. As I stated in Chapter three, the American Psychological Association is now requiring us as clinicians to recognize the importance of a client's spirituality. It is our responsibility to competently assess and address a client's unique spiritual religious beliefs and practices (SRBP), and the relevance spirituality has in relation to the presenting problem.

This is in large part due to the increase in demand on the part of clients to have their spirituality be an integral part of their treatment (Miller, 1999). Interestingly, the topic of addressing spirituality in psychotherapy has historically been a controversial topic in mainstream psychology. I believe this new directive on the part of the APA will change that since we cannot adequately carry out the APA's directive to address spirituality in treatment if we do not begin to identify and appropriate psycho-spiritual interventions to do this.

The work of Saunders, Miller, and Bright (2010) is recommended as a vital resource in understanding the topic of assessing and addressing a client's spirituality in treatment and how to do this with the APA's ethical guidelines in mind (I highly recommend reading the full article if you are interested in integrating Sozo into your clinical practice.

The authors identify a helpful continuum of care relating to spirituality.

Avoidant----------Conscious----------Integrated----------Directive

On one end of the continuum is spiritually avoidant care. This occurs when the clinician avoids issues related to a client's SRBP or desire to discuss SRBP in treatment. The APA has made it clear that this is not ethical especially when the individual is requesting it. On the other end of the continuum is spiritually directive care. There are specific situations in which this is indicated. The client must be explicitly asking for this level of spiritual intervention and the clinician must be competent to provide it. When operating under this level of care clinicians need to be especially careful to hold to professional role boundaries and maintain respect of the client's spirituality.

Most Christian psychology falls under spiritually integrated care. This level of spiritual and psychological intervention is necessary when working with "highly religious clients." In fact, the authors reference research that points to the lack of improvement on the part of highly religious clients when psychotherapy does not explicitly address treatment issues with their religious background in mind. In other words, for a devoted Christian seeking treatment, we as clinicians actually do them a disservice when we do not address their SRBP as part of their treatment. Finally, the authors point out that, "Psychologists should always engage, at the least, in spiritually conscious care with all patients" (p.355).

> One end of the continuum entails spiritually avoidant care, where the psychologist attempts to avoid issues related to a patient's SRBP. At its extreme, the psychologist avoids SRBP entirely, even when a patient indicates a need or desire to discuss them. At the other end of the continuum, spiritually directive psychotherapy is characterized by the psychotherapist's explicit and deliberate focus on the SRBP of patients, with the end goal of helping patients resolve psychological problems either by maintaining or transforming those beliefs and behaviors. Situated in between these approaches, spiritually integrated psychotherapy focuses on patients' SRBP but does not seek explicitly to either maintain or transform them. In this approach, SRBP may be the object of focus because they have a role in the cause, maintenance or amelioration of psychological problems, which are the primary focus of treatment. Finally, we suggest that psychologists should always engage, at the least, in spiritually conscious care with all patients. This entails assessing SRBP in a respectful and sensitive manner to determine their salience to the patient and the patient's problems. Spiritually conscious care entails its own ethical challenges, including being competent to recognize when a patient is in need of spiritually integrated or even spiritually directive psychotherapy and, if the psychologist cannot provide such care competently, how to refer appropriately (p.355).

Depending on how it is used (within the psychotherapy context or if a client is referred out) and the background and desire of the client, Sozo is a process by which counselors can engage their clients in "spiritually integrated, spiritually directive, or even spiritually conscious care."

Remember when Jenni re-entered treatment with me? She had two requests. The first was to "go to the next level" in her treatment for an eating disorder. The second was to "go to the next level" in her relationship with God. Responding to both of these requests required something more on the continuum of spiritually integrated to spiritually directive care. It falls somewhere within both of these modalities because there is overlap between spiritually directive and spiritually integrative psychotherapy. "The difference is in whether SRBP is the focus of change efforts. Because SRBP and psychological health are intimately interrelated, spiritually integrative psychotherapy may lead to change in a patient's SRBP (e.g., more frequent prayer)" (p.358). In other words, even when a clinician is not explicitly engaging in spiritually directive care, changes in beliefs may occur because our soul and spirits are intertwined.

Once again, following well-researched guidelines in terms of the integration of Christianity and Psychology is a given. The well-respected and renowned work of Dr. Mark McMinn (2012) thoroughly investigates and outlines guidelines for integrating faith, prayer, and Christian principles such as sin and forgiveness into psychotherapy. His book *Psychology, Theology, and Spirituality in Christian Counseling* (2012) is a helpful resource when generally considering the ethics and (contra)indications for using such things as prayer in counseling.

Attachment Theory

Currently, there is much discussion on the relationship between religiosity, spirituality, mental health, and healing. Many long-standing therapeutic models are being reevaluated within the context of religion or personal relationship with God. Attachment theory is one of the theories that has been deemed important in the discussion of spirituality and mental health. In 1969 John Bowlby described attachment as a lasting psychological connectedness between human beings (Bowlby, 1969, p.194). He believed that the earliest bonds formed by children with their caregivers have a tremendous impact that continues throughout life. Since that time, attachment theory has made a significant impact on the field of social, developmental, personality, and clinical psychology. (Reinsert & Edwards, 2009).

Attachment theory has also been studied in the context of religion and through the lens of God as the ideal, all-loving and nurturing attachment figure (Kirkpatrick, 1992). Research in this area directly supports the theory underlying the Father Ladder. Specifically, attachment research has shown that early childhood attachment to parents, either secure or insecure, directly relates to how a child views their relationship with God. (Kirkpatrick, 1992) (Granqvist, 1998) (Reinert & Edwards, 2009). If a child grows up with a secure attachment to their parents, than attachment to God will likely be secure; conversely, if the child grows up with an insecure attachment to their parents, than attachment to God will likely be insecure. (Granqvist & Hagekull, 1999). Granqvist's (1998) research showed that children who grow up with an insecure relationship with nonreligious parents will often turn to God later in
life, while those who grew up with an insecure relationship with very re-

ligious parents will often turn away from God and the religion they were raised in. When childhood abuse is factored into the equation, one's view of God tends to be even more negative (Kennedy & Drebing, 2002), but in some instances when sexual abuse has occurred and there is evidence of trauma, subjects still seem to be spiritually thriving. (Reinert & Bloomingdale, 1999). Beginning with Kirkpatrick (2005), we have come to understand and study attachment theory as a critical aspect in understanding relationships to God and that this idea is observed cross-culturally (e.g., Rohner, 1986). Kirkpatrick theorizes that an individual's perception of God is the single most critical aspect in defining their other attachment relationships. Individuals with insecure attachments displayed insecure attachments with God, while those with secure loving attachments viewed God as loving and caring. Kirkpatrick calls this the "correspondence hypothesis" that leads to the "compensation hypothesis". Sozo is a tool that is consistent with both hypotheses.

From a psychological perspective Sozo helps to identify unhealthy attachments in order to provide a new healthier attachment with the

Godhead. This is what Kirkpatrick called "surrogate attachment." This means that when poorly secured individuals are able to connect with God in a meaningful way, they are able to experience an inner sense of security. God can then compensate for the individual's unhealthy attachment by meeting the needs that were not met in childhood (compensation hypothesis).

"Human beings are biologically primed to seek moral and spiritual meaning, and nurturing relationships are a central foundation for positive moral and spiritual development" (Benson et al, 2003). We are created for relationship with both people and God. When our dysfunctional attachments become a determinant in how we view God, Sozo and the Father Ladder tool can be used to heal those detriments and promote healthy spiritual development.

Prayer and Forgiveness

The use of prayer in counseling has been a controversial issue in mainstream psychology and there are some that argue that it should not be used in psychotherapy at all. Other research suggests that "prayer can be integrated in a sensitive, natural, and careful manner that has largely been helpful to the therapeutic process" (Gubi, 2009, p.120).

In recent years, many lay Christian counseling models and inner healing techniques and deliverance methods have evolved and received both empirical support and criticism concurrently. Experts in the field of integration of Christianity and psychology continue to study the impact that lay Christian counseling has had on professional Christian counseling. "Historically, ministry or pastoral care has been "based chiefly on reflection and deduction from principles derived from Scripture and pastoral experience, whereas modern psychologies, while also indebted to reflection and theorizing, are grounded more in behavioral science investigation characterized by inductive, empirical study" (Yarhouse, Butman, & McRay, 2005, p.16). Researchers in this area have pointed out that this "disparity in approaches often creates tension when the two horizons attempt to meet and explore areas of integration, and much of the tension appears to arise from differing epistemological postures" (Hunter, 2009). As Christian psychologists we are continually challenged and responsible to "maintain the authority of scripture yet remain committed to a discipline that utilizes a radically different epistemology" (Hill, 2005, p.98).

Siang-Yan Tan (2005) who is both a licensed clinical psychologist and an ordained pastor, subscribes to an epistemological approach that integrates understanding both the Scripture and psychological findings. He states that while it is crucial for him to "depend on the Holy Spirit and His anointing in studying the biblical texts or Scriptures," he is not hesitant in "citing relevant research to support and expand on biblical truths." Careful to use "sound exegesis and biblical interpretation," Tan also draws from core psychological concepts to assist others in viewing "human beings from a more comprehensive perspective" (p.50-51).

An article by Garzon, Worthington, and Tan (2009) is perhaps the most comprehensive examination of current Christian lay counseling models to date. They suggest four classifications of lay Christian counseling models: Active Listening approaches, Cognitive and Solution-Focused approaches, Inner Healing approaches, and Mixed approaches. The authors point out that inner healing is different from the other approaches they classified in that it "emphasizes prayer-filled encounters with Christ as the change mechanism instead of therapist-mediated or psychological theory-derived activities. Some techniques appear (to most professionals) to be similar to psychodynamic and experiential psychotherapies; however, inner healing emphasizes prayer-filled encounters with Christ as the change mechanism instead of therapist-mediated or psychological theory-derived activities." (p.115).

Investigation into the credibility of current inner healing methods has shown some positive results (Garzon & Burket, 2002; McCullough, Worthington, & Rachel, 1997). At the heart of current Inner Healing Pray (IHP) methods like Sozo are the core Christian concepts of prayer and forgiveness. Forgiveness is a key principle in the Sozo ministry. Many psychological studies have shown forgiveness to be a powerful component in psychological and physical health. Pioneers in this area of research include Robert D. Enright and Everett Worthington who founded the Campaign for Forgiveness Research. Studies on the topic have shown the power of forgiveness to positively affect heart disease, crime prevention, troubled marriages, family dynamics, and even international conflict. Enright and Coyle (1998) report that, "Forgiveness may be taught and learned, and that the outcomes can be quite favorable." Across all of the studies, there was not one instance in which a group experiencing forgiveness education showed a decline in psychological health. In fact, statistically significant improvement in such variables as hope and self-esteem, as well as significant decreases in anxiety and depression, were more the rule than the exception."

Enright (2001) developed "the process model of forgiving," an early intervention to promote forgiveness. Phases in this model include the "uncovering, decision, work, and outcome/deepening phase." In the uncovering phase, the unjust injury to the individual is identified and the related painful emotions are experienced. In the decision phase, the individual begins to understand that additional healing may be compromised unless a decision is made to surrender and a "heart conversion" or life change occurs. In the work phase, the individual begins to develop a new understanding of the injurer. "The work phase also includes the heart of forgiveness which is the acceptance of the pain that resulted from the actions of the injurer." And, finally, in the outcome/deepening phase,

> ... the forgiving individual begins to realize that he/she is gaining emotional relief from the process of forgiving his/her injurer. The forgiving individual may find meaning in the suffering that he/she has faced. The emotional relief and new-found meaning may lead to increased compassion for self and others. The individual may discover a new purpose in life and an active concern for his/her community. Thus, the forgiver discovers the paradox of forgiveness: as we give to others the gifts of mercy, generosity, and moral love, we ourselves are healed. (Enright and Coyle, 1998, p.139).

Similarly, Sozo appears to guide an individual through all four of these phases quickly. Because it relies on the movement of Holy Spirit in an individual's heart and mind, Sozo may speed up the forgiveness process without compromising the depth of the healing and forgiveness.

Final Thoughts

I believe that by integrating Sozo with research-based clinical modalities in therapeutic settings, we will see more people restored to wholeness as they heal their connection with God. I have found that by using this approach and helping to deepen that connection, the transformation and healing of psychological issues is brought about in greater depth and wholeness than previously seen with traditional Christian or secular psychology. Through the partnership of truths from the world of psychology and those from the world of inner healing, we can see powerful healing and transformation occur. While the Sozo tools have not been studied in an empirical manner, the principles and tools are consistent with Christian psychology and I look forward to future research focusing on this powerful tool.

It is a privilege to be able to introduce Sozo to the field of Christian psychology and train therapists to create a sacred space for the ultimate soul-ologist and Overseer of souls to come in and help our clients. The healing we offer as Christian therapists is for body, soul, and spirit and the author and provider of that healing is God.

For "you were like sheep going astray,"

but now you have returned

to the Shepherd and

Overseer of your souls.

F.A.Q

Sozo Training Guidelines for those in the Mental Health Fields

Q. Is Sozo a tool that I can use in professional settings?

Sozo is a powerful tool that can be been used by Christian mental health professionals and students of psychology, counseling, social work, and associated fields. It is encouraged that if you are going to use Sozo in these settings, that you hold true to the model and use it the way that it was intended. This usually means referring the person out for a Sozo session at a local ministry, or holding a separate session designated for Sozo in your practice. Informed consent is very important when doing Sozo in a professional setting. Clients should be given full informed consent and made aware of the fact that Sozo was NOT developed NOT as a professional counseling tool. Clients should also be given the option of doing the Sozo session with their counselor, or with an outside ministry team. Once the client has underwent a Sozo, the Sozo tools can be integrated within the session for ongoing work and for addressing new wounds and lies that may emerge.

Following well-researched guidelines in terms of the integration of Christianity and Psychology is also necessary. Psychology, Theology, and Spirituality in Christian Counseling by Dr. Mark McMinn is a recommended resource.

Q. How do I document a Sozo session?

Here is an example of a session note that could be used to document Jenni's Sozo session.

<u>Session Note: Jenni K.   3/4/2009</u>

Client engaged in identifying and processing wounds connected to her family of origin and related contributions to cognitive distortions surrounding the client's eating disorder.

Utilized the client's SRBP as a strength-based resource in reframing maladaptive cognitions by having the client identify how her faith informs her in regards to positively changing her maladaptive beliefs. Utilized prayer and forgiveness as a spiritual resource to connect the client with her Higher Power.

Client was able to feel a sense of spiritual comfort and guidance in connecting with her Higher Power and reframing cognitions. She responded positively reporting new insight into the psychological and spiritual contributors to her problem and supportive connection with her Higher Power. She displayed appropriate cognitive and emotional connection to new healthier cognitions.

Next session: Process/identify how client will employ healthier coping behaviors that are inline with today's new insights and how she can continue to benefit from her spiritual resources.

Q. Are there Sozo trainings geared towards professionals in the field?

Yes, Sozo trainings geared especially for mental health professionals and students are given upon request by Dr. Margaret Nagib, clinical psychologist, who oversees Sozo in these professional arenas. For more information go to bethelsozo.com/margaret-nagib or Dr. Nagib's website at thedunamisproject.org

Q. What about Sozo trainings not given by Dr. Nagib? Can I still benefit from those?

Sozo trainings given by other certified Sozo trainers are just as beneficial but do not address the unique questions that professionals in the field may have about Sozo and its use.

Q. What happens after I attend a Sozo training?

Once trained, it is very important to follow the guidelines of Bethel Sozo (see website or manual) regarding, training, mentoring, and spiritual covering. If you have just been trained in Sozo and would like to utilize Sozo, it is important that you receive mentoring from the team that trained you, or partner with an established Sozo ministry to gain competence in Sozo before using it in your practice or ministry. If you plan on using Sozo in your professional practice or facility, it is important to get the approval of your direct supervisor and/or the facilities clinical director (and the client) before using Sozo. The client can also be referred out for a session.

Q. The ministry model involves having two additional individuals in the session to provide intercessory prayer (they are called the "Second" and the "Third"). If I am a licensed professional, can I do Sozo without prayer intercessors?

Yes, if you are licensed. Although, counselors may consider including an intercessor such as a professional colleague who is also trained in Sozo. Some counselors have preferred to be the Second and sit in on their client's Sozo at a local ministry. If Seconds are used in the professional setting, it is very important to follow the APA guidelines for informed consent and confidentiality. Do not force your client to have a Second if they are not comfortable with this.

Q. How about graduate students or other unlicensed persons?

Graduate students are advised to come under the covering of a local ministry to be mentored and gain competence. In short, students and professionals should follow the Bethel Sozo guidelines for training and mentoring.

Q. Does Dr. Nagib provide supervision for professionals?

Yes, individual and group supervision, Sozo mentoring, and trainings are available.

Q. How about Shabar/Advanced Sozo?

Once again, Bethel Sozo guidelines should be followed in regards to when an individual is ready to go through advanced and Shabar training. Irrespective of any prior professional training in the area of DID and related issues, Shabar training should only be attended when the individual has met the prerequisites as outlined by Bethel Sozo.

Once a person has undergone the training, mentoring in this area is especially important. Shabar should not be used in a professional setting without your supervisor's approval and without informed consent of the client. Once again, Shabar was designed as a ministry tool and not a counseling tool and this should be made known to the client before use.

*Always abide by your state licensure board's ethical and professional guidelines and the guidelines for your professional community (APA, etc) when using Sozo or Shabar as an auxiliary tool in professional settings.

REFERENCES

Benson, P.L., Roehlkepartain, E.C., & Rude, S.P. (2003). Spiritual development in childhood and adolescence: Toward a field of inquiry. Applied developmental science, 7, 204–212.

Bowlby, J. (1969). Attachment and loss. Attachment. New York, NY: Basic Books.

Bretherton. I., (1992) The origins of attachment theory: John Bowlby and Mary Einsworth. Developmental psychology 28, 759-775.

Bryner, J., Wang, U., Hui, J., Bedodo, M., MacDougall, C., & Anderson, I. (2006). Dextromethorphan abuse in adolescence, an increasing trend: 1999-2004. Archives of pediatric and adolescent medicine. http://archpedi.ama-ssn.org/cgi/reprint/160/12/1217

DeSilva, D. & Liebscher, T. (2004). Sozo: Saved healed and delivered training manual. Redding, CA: Bethel Church.

Enright, R. (2001). Forgiveness is a choice. Washington, DC: APA Books.

Enright, R., Freedman, S., & Rique, J. (1998). The psychology of interpersonal forgiveness.Exploring forgiveness. 46-62. Madison, WI: University of Wisconsin Press.

Enright, R.D. & Coyle, C.T. (1998). Researching the process model of forgiveness within psychological interventions. In Dimensions of forgiveness: Psychological research & theological forgiveness, ed. Worthington, Jr., E.L. (1998). 139-161.

Garzon, F., (2005). Inner healing prayer in "spirit-filled" Christianity. Faculty publications and Presentations, 40, 148-159.

Garzon, F., & Burkett, L., (2002). Healing of memories: models, research, future directions. Journal of psychology and Christianity, 21(1), 42-49.

Garzon, F., & Poloma, M. (2005). Theophostic ministry: preliminary practitioner survey. Pastoral psychology, 53, 387-396.

Garzon, F., & Tilley, K. (2009). Do lay Christian counseling approaches work? What we currently know. Journal of Psychology and Christianity, 28,130-140.

Garzon, F., Worthington, E. L., & Tan, S. (n.d.). (2009). Lay christian counseling and client expectations for integration in therapy. Journal of Psychology and Christianity, 28(2), 113-120.

Gassin, E., & Enright, R. (1995). The will to meaning in the process of forgiveness. Journal of psychology and Christianity, 14, 38-49.

Granqvist, P. (1998). Religiousness and perceived childhood attachment: on the question of compensation or correspondence. Journal for the scientific study of religion, 37, 350-367.

Granqvist P., & Hagekull, B., (1999). Religiousness and perceived childhood attachment: profiling socialized correspondence and emotional compensation. Journal for the scientific study of religion, 38, 254-273.

Granqvist, P., Ivarsson, T., Broberg, A.G., & Hagekull, B. (2007). Examining relations among attachment, religiosity, and new age spirituality using the Adult Attachment Interview. Developmental psychology, 43(3), 590-601.

Guzik, D. (2011). Study Guide for 1 Thessalonians 5. Enduring Word Commentary Series. Blue Letter Bible (www.blueletterbible.org).

Gubi, P. M. (2009). A qualitative exploration into how the use of prayer in counseling and psychotherapy might be ethically problematic. Counseling and Psychotherapy Research, 9(2), 115-121.

Hambrick, D., & Fredrickson, J. (2001). Are you sure you have a strategy? Academy of management executive 15(4), 48-59.

Hatch, M.J., & Cunliffe, A. (2006). Organization theory. New York, NY: Oxford University Press.

Hunter, L. (2009). Epistemological approaches to inner healing and integration. Journal of Psychology and Christianity, 28(2), 101-104.

Kennedy, P., & Drebing, C. (2002). Abuse and religious experience: A study of religiously committed evangelical adults. Mental health, religion and culture, 5, 225-237.

Kirkpatrick, L.A., & Shaver, P.R. (1990). Attachment theory and religion: Childhood attachments, religious beliefs and conversions. Journal for the scientific study of religion,29, 315-334.

Kirkpatrick, L.A. (1992). An attachment-theory approach to the psychology of religion. International journal for the psychology of religion, 2, 3.

Kirkpatrick, L.A. (2005). Attachment, evolution, and the psychology of religion. New York, NY:Guilford Press.

McCullough, M.E., Worthington, L.R., & Rachel, K.C. (1997). Interpersonal forgiving in close relationships. Journal of personality and social psychology. 73(2), 321-336.

McMinn, M. (2012). Psychology, theology, and spirituality in christian counseling. Carol Stream, IL: Tyndale House.

Monroe, P. G., & Schwab, G. M. (2009). God as healer: A closer look at biblical images of inner healing with guided questions for counselors . Journal of Psychology and Christianity, 28(2), 121-129.

Nagib, M.N., Miller, K. (2012). Strengthening the spirit and restoring the soul. identifying, understanding and healing the blocks with the father, son and holy spirit. The Journal of Christian Healing, Volume 28, #1, Spring/Summer, 2012. 61

Nee, W., (1968). The spiritual man. New York, NY: Christian Fellowship Publishers Inc.

Pargament, K.I., & Saunders, S.M. (2007). Introduction to the special issue on spirituality and psychotherapy. Journal of clinical psychology, 63, 903-907.

Pargament, K. (March, 2013 22). what role do religion and spirituality play in mental health?. Retrieved from http://www.apa.org/news/press/releases/2013/03/religion-spirituality.aspx

Rainey, C.A. (2008). Are individual forgiveness interventions for adults more effective than group interventions? A meta-analysis. (Doctoral dissertation). California Polytechnic University.

Reinert, D., & Bloomingdale, J. (1999). Spiritual maturity and mental health: Implications for counseling. Counseling & values, 43, 211-223.

Reinert, D., & Edwards, C. (2009). Attachment theory, childhood mistreatment, and religiosity. Psychology of religion and spirituality. 1(1), 25-34.

Rohner, R. P. (1986). The warmth dimension. London, UK: Sage.

Saunders, S.M., Miller M., & Bright, M., (2010). Spiritually conscious psychological care. Psychology: Research and practice, 41(5), 355-362.

Seamonds, D., (1988) Healing grace. Wheaton, IL: Victor Books.

Smith, E.M. (2005). Healing life's hurts through Theophostic Prayer: Let the light of Christ set you free from lifelong fears, shame, false guilt, anxiety and emotional pain. New Creation Publishing.

Toussaint, L., & Webb, J. (2005). The assessment of multiple dimensions of forgiveness. Paper presented at the 78th Annual Conference of the Midwestern Psychological Association, Chicago, IL.

Vallotton, K., Johnson, B., (2006). The supernatural ways of royalty. Shipensburgh, PA: Destiny Image Publishers, Inc.

Walker, D., Reese, J., Hughes, J., & Troskie, M. (2010). Addressing religious and spiritual issues in trauma-focused cognitive behavior therapy for children and adolescents. Professional psychology: Research and practice, 40(2), 174-180.

Webb, J., Robinson, E., & Brower, K. (2011). Mental health, not social support, mediates the forgiveness-alcohol outcome relationship. Psychology of addictive behaviors. Vol 25(3),462-473.

Wolk, A., & Kreitz, K., (2008). Business planning for enduring social impact: A social entrepreneurial approach to solving social problems. Cambridge, MA: Root Cause.

Worthington, E.L.Jr. (1998). Dimensions of forgiveness: Psychological research & theological forgiveness. Templeton Foundation Press.

Worthington, E.L. Jr., Berry, J.W., & Parrott, L., III. (2001). Unforgiveness, forgiveness, religion and health In T.G. Plante & A.C. Sherman (EDs.), Faith and health: Psychological perspectives (p. 107-138) New York, NY: Guilford Press.

Worthington, E. L. Jr., (2006). Forgiveness intervention manuals. Retrieved from http://www.people.vcu.edu/~eworth/

Wu, L., Pillowsky, D., & Patkar, A. (2007). Non-prescribed use of pain relievers among adolescents in the United States. Drug and alcohol dependence. 94(1-3), 1-11.

Yarhouse, M. A., Butman, R. E., & McRay, B. W. (2005). Modern psychopathologies: A comprehensive Christian appraisal. Downers Grove, IL: InterVarsity.

Printed in Great Britain
by Amazon